The Unseen Path

Nagababu Jannu

Copyright

This memoir is based on the author's personal experiences. Certain names, places, and identifying details have been changed to protect the privacy of individuals. The events and conversations are recalled to the best of the author's memory.

First edition: 2026

Published by: Nagababu Jannu

ISBN: 978-93-5655-407-8

India

Foreword

God creates each one of us with immense potential to achieve meaningful goals in life. Though our journeys may begin with uncertainty, faith, struggle, and patience gradually reveal a clear path forward. *The Unseen Path* reflects one such journey; quiet, courageous, and deeply inspiring.

Being a mother first and a teacher later, I have personally witnessed the inner strength of those around me, and I take pride in being a part of their growth and transformation.

Born into a family grounded in empathy and values, Nagababu rose in life with dignity and independence intact. Despite the obstacles he faced, he embraced them as opportunities, with support from family, friends, and mentors who believed in him.

The Unseen Path reminds us that true ability often lies beyond what we see. When determination is strong, support arrives in unexpected ways.

I hope this autobiography inspires many by highlighting the perseverance and potential of the differently abled.

- Swarnalatha (teacher)

Author's Note

Every event and emotion in this book is drawn from my real life. While a few names have been adjusted for privacy, every struggle, victory, and moment of transformation described here happened as I remember it.

The legal judgments and government orders I mention in the book may seem small, but they marked the first breakthroughs. I hope these steps help light the way, both for those who will walk this path and for those already finding their way along it.

I've written this book with the same tools that helped me study and work: a screen reader, a keyboard, and faith. The faith in God, in myself, and in the purpose of my journey.

I've always believed that there is a divine reason behind every challenge. This belief has given me the strength to move forward, even when the path seemed impossible.

What you will read is not a story of disability, but of determination lived fully, remembered deeply, and shared truthfully.

If this book helps even one person believe in their unseen strength, its purpose will be fulfilled.

Editorial Acknowledgement

I thank Shikha Thakur and Rebecca Malachi for shaping this manuscript into a refined book with patience, insight, and editorial excellence. The effort, research, and interactions that went into this work extended far beyond editing.

Preface

Writing *The Unseen Path* was not just an act of memory; it was an act of faith in God's plan, my own purpose, and every challenge of my life. Every word you are about to read was written without sight, but never without vision.

I wrote this book with the same patience that once helped me learn Braille. I used the JAWS (Job Access With Speech) screen reader and a standard keyboard, which are the main tools for blind users. I composed, corrected, and rebuilt every line only through listening and re-listening until my story found its rhythm.

This process was more than writing; it was rebuilding life through my memories and feelings.

Each chapter carries a trace of memory, the warmth of my mother's hands, the voices of teachers who believed in me, the quiet support of my friends, and the echo of footsteps that taught me where hope begins.

I did not write this book to prove what a blind person can do, but to show what any person can do when they refuse to not give up.

This book took shape slowly, through nights of recalling events, re-listening to old recordings, and reliving moments that once tested my strength but later revealed purpose.

Introduction

Every life has a rhythm; sometimes clear, sometimes silent, sometimes waiting to be heard.

Mine began in darkness, but it was never without direction. The moment I was born, the room held more questions than joy; fear and disbelief of my family and people in the hospital filled the air.

I wrote The Unseen Path to share the journey of finding strength when the road itself seemed invisible. It is a story of belief that grows from faith, resilience, and the will to move forward despite uncertainty.

For most of my life, the path ahead revealed itself only when I started walking. Every stage, from classrooms that tested my patience to the fight for my right to study engineering, prepared me for greater challenges in finding a place in the leading global technology firms.

Back then, around 2010, diversity & inclusion (D&I) barely existed in the Indian work environment. Adapting to the tools and work environments they had was another challenge. Most people had a perception that the blind cannot lead teams, make strategic decisions, and manage tech projects. So I had to prove again and again that my capability is not defined by sight but by vision. All these became my stepping stones to what I am today.

Every chapter is a reminder that strength does not come from what we are given, but from what we create out of it. That's The Unseen Path.

Welcome to my journey, a road that was never found but forged.

I want readers, especially parents, to stop focusing on what their children lack and start seeing the spark that makes them unique. With the right support and encouragement, that spark can turn into something extraordinary.

As you turn the pages, you will meet people with caring hearts, helping hands, and encouraging voices who became my compass to navigate life. I want my readers to understand that life, no matter how ordinary or overlooked, holds an extraordinary purpose waiting to unfold.

Prologue: Born against the odds

Everything I know about the day I was born lives in the stories my mother and grandparents told me. They described it so vividly that it feels as though I was there myself.

It was the summer of June 8, 1986, in Vuyyuru, a small town in Andhra Pradesh, India, where my story began. I was told that the day was so hot that even the wind refused to move. The sun pressed hard against tiled roofs, and the air hung thick with dust.

Outside Pinamaneni Nursing Home, a modest hospital in the heart of the town, vendors called out for snacks and cool drinks, their voices blending with the hum of the afternoon.

But inside, everything slowed down. Footsteps, voices, and even breaths slowed down, as if the air itself had grown heavy.

The hospital smelled of Dettol, spirit, and phenyl. Ceiling fans groaned overhead, stirring the warm air but offering no comfort. People waited on wooden benches, their murmurs rising and falling like waves on a distant shore.

My father, Nancharaiah, waited outside the operation theater, anxious and silent. Even my maternal uncles, Venkateshwarao and Pattabi, and paternal uncles, Durgarao and Sambhasivarao, were with him.

My father worked as a cycle mechanic and was known for his skills with machines and quick hands. He was not bad at heart, but drinking too often took hold of his better side at times, turning some days unpredictable.

However, that day, he was quiet, hopeful, and sober.

My maternal grandfather, Gurunadham, sat with his head bowed, whispering mantras under his breath. He had never gone to school, yet he carried himself with dignity. He ran a small cool drink shop and was respected in our town for his honesty and self-discipline. To him, work was worship.

My grandmother, Anasurya, who believed that prayers could do wonders, started praying softly, "Swamy Rakshinchandi." It is a Telugu plea that means "Lord, protect them," often spoken in moments of fear. She had no formal education, but her faith was deep and unwavering.

My paternal grandparents, Ramayya and Chayamma, were silent, yet I'm told they were steady with fear and hope.

And in the center of all was my mother, Venkateshwaramma. Kind-hearted and spiritual, she was a woman of calm that always steadied everyone around her. Her prayers had no script, they were born from love and strength.

Behind the closed doors of the operation theater, my mother was fighting her own battle. Hours of labor had left her weak, yet she held on to every breath. The labor wasn't progressing normally, and there were growing concerns about her condition and mine. Doctors decided that a cesarean section was the only way to bring me safely into the world.

I have been told this story many times by my mother, how metal instruments clinked against steel trays, nurses hurried across the floor, and the air was heavy with the smell of antiseptic. It was a scene I have learned to imagine through their stories.

My mother's strength was fading, yet she held on.

Then came my first cry, a sharp, insistent sound that cut through the stillness of the room.

Outside, in the waiting hall, relief spread like cool air after a long, hot day.

My grandmother gasped, “Babu vachhadu,” which means, “Our boy is here.”

But inside, under the bright glare of the theater lamps, the doctor examined me carefully. He moved a small torch in front of my eyes.

No response.

He tried again. Still nothing.

A quiet understanding passed his face.

He stepped out, his voice heavy as he said to my father, “Your son is blind.”

And for a moment, everything fell silent.

My father froze. My grandparents stood still.

Then came the whispers from the people who were around, in the hospital corridor. Soft. Relentless. “A blind child… what life will he ever have?” “He will end up begging.” “This is a curse on the family.”

On the hospital bed, pale and trembling, my mother heard every one of them. She had endured pain, fear, and exhaustion, and now the sharper sting of fate.

Between fear and faith, something in her spirit refused to break. Through the pain and tears, she made a vow; fierce, silent, and unshakable.

"My son will not beg. He will not live in shame. Even if I must stand against the world, I will make him walk with dignity."

That vow, which was born in the sterile air of an operation theater, became the shield I have carried all my life. It was my mother's first gift to me. And it has never left my side.

Chapter 1: Fragile bonds, unbreakable will

Everything I remember about my early childhood comes from the small mud-floored house in Vuyyuru. We lived there with my maternal grandparents.

It was the late 1980s, a time when electricity came and went like a passing thought. And the slow whirring of the ceiling fan felt like luxury.

The floor was uneven and cool beneath my feet, from years of being swept and sprinkled with water to settle the dust.

Mornings carried their own music and embrace. The smell of tamarind rice mixed with the smoke of firewood curling up from the kitchen. And the soft humming of my mother that woke me every morning.

Followed by the voices of chickens clucking somewhere outside my room's window, the faint calls of neighbors across low mud walls, and the clear, steady sound of a temple bell at dawn that woke the town.

I was breathing through the rhythm of daily sounds and the warmth of familiar hands of my mother and grandmother.

When the power failed in the evenings, I could tell by the shift in the air. The sudden stillness, the quiet gasp from someone, and the faint rustle as lamps were lit. The room felt gentler then, as if even sound had lowered its voice.

I often sat close to my grandmother during evenings, her saree smelling faintly of soap and turmeric. She narrated to me stories of gods and demons in a steady, lilting voice.

My grandfather spoke less, but his voice was calm and firm, like a drumbeat. His few words anchored me even when I couldn't yet understand their full meaning.

He often said, "Never think about what you don't have; think about what you can do with what you have."

And when I hesitated or withdrew in silence, he would place his hand gently on my shoulder and say, "The world listens only to those who speak through their actions."

Those words sank deeper than I realized then. Even today, they echo within me, guiding me through uncertainties, reminding me to keep moving forward.

He always took me along wherever he went, holding my hand firmly through crowds. With him, I felt seen, not for what I lacked, but for what I could become.

We had simple meals, mostly rice with slurry dal, lentil soup that is a staple in every Indian household. Sometimes, there was chutney, a vegetable dip, to make the food go down easier. Clothes were patched until there was barely any fabric left to patch.

From what I vaguely recollect, life was not easy, yet I felt safe within those walls, protected by the warmth of my grandmother's presence and my mother's quiet determination.

Every afternoon, my cousins pulled me into their games. Sometimes they treated me no differently, and at times they left me out in awkward silence.

At that age, I only knew that something set me apart. Yet I didn't know how deeply it ran.

Blindness had touched my family long before it touched me. From my mother's side, it had been present for generations. An unspoken thread through our bloodline. It is a common practice in some communities of South India to marry cousins. They did not recognize that this shared lineage would one day shape the course of my life.

Blindness, in those days, was considered not another way of living but the end of living itself.

Yet my parents refused to accept that fate. They chased every possibility of restoring my sight. They consulted Dr. Shiva Reddy, a renowned ophthalmologist of his time. After careful examination, he told them that nothing more could be done.

Still, my parents did not stop trying. When I was 5, they took me to meet a Swamiji, a mystic who was believed to have miraculous healing powers.

I remember the rattle of the train tracks, the smell of metal and steam, and my mother's anxious grip on my hand, as it was the first train journey of my life.

But even there, nothing changed. They returned with heavy hearts, but without regret. Their efforts were their way of fighting for me long before I had the strength to fight for myself.

As I grew older, I often overheard whispers of my relatives while they thought I wasn't listening. "This boy is blind. What future will he ever have?"

Those voices shaped my earliest memories, voices that defined what I could not be. I couldn't see their faces, but I felt the weight of their words.

At that age, I had no answers but feelings. Feelings of confusion, isolation, and the ache of being judged. These were too big of emotions for a child to name.

And yet, somewhere deep inside, without knowing how or why, a spark began to grow. A quiet certainty that this would not be my story.

But I didn't only grow up with the weight of blindness. I was battling two other worries as well. One was poverty, a constant factor pressed into every meal, every decision, every dream.

The other was my father's drinking habits. Unpredictable, heavy, and a concern always waiting at the door. He was trapped in a habit that stole his peace and ours.

Back then, it shaped my childhood. Even today, the struggle remains the same. And I stand where my mother once stood, carrying the family financially, holding together what might otherwise fall apart.

It was not just blindness I had to rise against. It was circumstance. It was instability. It was everything that said our lives could only remain as they were.

Home was not always peaceful.

Some nights he came home quietly, ate his food, and slept; those were calm nights. But on other nights, the smell of liquor arrived before he did. That was the warning of the storm to come.

The first sign was the uneven thud of his footsteps. The door would slam open. Vessels clattered. His voice rose louder. “Why isn’t the food ready? What is this mess?”

Even when the food had been waiting, the words still came.

My mother never shouted back. She silently served food and took the blows as they came.

I remember one night clearly. The sharp sound of his hand striking her cheek. Her muffled cry. The crash of bangles scattering across the floor.

I crouched in a corner, my hands over my ears.

My grandmother pulled me close, whispering, "Nothing happened, Nani… it will pass." She always called me Nani, a Telugu word of affection for a child.

But how could a child close his ears to the trouble inside his own home?

The following morning, my mother rose as if nothing had happened. It was like any other day for her. I could hear the sound of utensils in the kitchen and the steady click-clack of her sewing machine that filled the room, the sound of her resilience.

She stitched cloth bags until her fingers ached, her eyes heavy from sleepless nights.

Each bag fetched only a few coins, but to me they meant much more. They were proof that she refused to give up. Her will stitched into every seam.

I often sat beside her, tracing the rough fabric with my fingers, listening to the rattle of the machine. To me it was more than sound; it was her heartbeat, steady and unbroken, carrying us forward.

I didn't know it then, but that was my first lesson in what strength truly sounds like.

I didn't have many toys, but the few I had were treasures. Two matchboxes tied with a string became my telephone. A small mirror, tilted to catch sunlight, became my game.

At that time, I could still see faint shades and light, and that moving patch of brightness fascinated me. I would sit for hours, tilting the mirror this way and that, watching the glow dance across the wall.

Those small inventions were my joys, and through them I discovered that imagination could be richer than any shop-bought toy.

Still, the reality around us was fragile.

My parents' marriage was like a clay pot veined with cracks. It could break any day, yet it didn't.

My mother never left, no matter how many times she was hurt. Perhaps it was love. Perhaps duty. Or perhaps that unbreakable vow to hold the family together.

Whatever the reason, I knew one thing, no matter what happened, I could lean on her.

In 1991, when I was 5, my paternal grandmother Chayamma passed away. It was my first encounter with death.

Death was a feeling I could not comprehend back then, but I could sense it in every sound and scent that filled our home.

The wailing of women, the smell of camphor and incense, the hushed voices of adults speaking in grief, and the silence that remained after rituals.

The house felt emptier, as if someone had demolished a strong pillar.

I did not spend much time with her, but I knew Chayamma was gentle and affectionate. She often told me about my father's childhood whenever we met. I still remember her voice, which was a beautiful blend of memory and laughter.

I didn't understand her stories back then, but she made me feel safe, as though I belonged to something larger than myself.

I didn't yet understand the meaning of forever, but I knew she was gone. Yet her presence remained, a soft echo in my earliest memories, teaching me before I could put my feelings into words.

Amid grief, whispers, and hardships, life went on.

To lift my mood, my mother sometimes took me to the cinema hall.

The bright lights, the loud sounds, and the crowd, all of it overwhelmed me. I often cried, tugging at her hand, begging to go home.

I don't know why, but the world outside felt harsher, louder, and less kind. All I ever wanted was to be in the comfort of my grandmother's lap.

No matter how hard life pressed, my mother never loosened her hold on that vow.

She kept it alive through her actions each day. Through every stitch, every tear she hid, and every meal she made. Though I was too young to grasp the weight of her struggle, her willpower wrapped me like armor.

By the time I turned 6, I had learned what was missing in my life.

But I had also learned something greater. That real strength does not always shout.

Sometimes it whispers. Sometimes it moves with the rhythm of a sewing machine. And sometimes it hides in the quiet embrace of a mother who refuses to break.

That was my lesson about resilience.

Our lives were fragile, but my mother's will was unbreakable. And that made me more determined. And that quiet strength became the first promise I made to myself that I would find my way, no matter how dark it seemed.

Chapter 2: First steps into education

As one chapter of my childhood quietly closed, another began. It was 1992 when my world shifted.

Until then, life had unfolded gently in the narrow lanes of Vuyyuru, under the care of my maternal grandparents. Their home had been my universe. A world of warmth, safety, and familiar sounds.

As I turned 6, our days began to tighten under the weight of financial strain. My father's income as a cycle mechanic was never enough. Moreover, his drinking habits made things worse. My mother stitched cloth bags for small shops. She tried to make the little she earned stretch into meals for three.

I could feel the silences deepen between my parents. Even as a child, I sensed something was changing. But I couldn't understand.

One evening, I overheard a quiet but serious conversation between my parents in the corner of our small house. By the end of it, they decided to leave Vuyyuru for Hyderabad, which was then the capital city of Andhra Pradesh. Currently, Hyderabad is the capital of Telangana state.

My mother believed that a city might offer better chances, not only for work but also for livelihood. For me, it meant stepping into a world I couldn't imagine. But the thought was frightening and exciting at the same time.

I didn't understand that we were parting with more than a house. We were leaving behind the comfort of my grandparents' home, the smell of tamarind rice from our kitchen, and the gentle murmur of my grandmother's evening prayers.

We packed our belongings and boarded a crowded bus to Hyderabad. The ride felt endless. Dust blew through the open windows. By the time we reached the city, the world had grown noisier.

The city had its own heartbeat. Bus horns, rushing crowds, and the constant rhythm of traffic that never seemed to rest. The air smelled different too. A mix of fried snacks and petrol fumes.

My maternal aunt, Rajini Kumari, welcomed us into her home. Her warmth felt like a soft bridge between the world we had left behind and the one we were stepping into. She had two daughters whose laughter filled every corner of the house.

I remember the scent of incense and the clatter of kitchen utensils. These sounds slowly made the city feel less strange. Both my aunt and her husband became our pillars during that time. Their constant support made it possible for my parents to dream again.

While we were settling down, my uncle opened a door that my parents had never imagined. He planted the first seed of hope as he told of a school for blind children, Darulshifa Blind Boys' High School.

Until then, the thought of me studying had felt distant, almost impossible. In Vuyyuru, people mostly spoke about my blindness as a burden, but my uncle's words carried a positive light. For the first time, someone used the words "Nagababu" and "education" together. It was like hearing my name tied to a purpose.

Before admitting me to school, my parents rented a single small room. That room became our whole universe.

I still remember it had a tiny window that never let enough light in, but it was ours, so it felt good. The cement floor under my bare feet felt cool in the mornings and warm by night.

A damaged sink clung to a wall, a few vessels stacked beside it, and above them hung a string that served as a clothesline.

At night, we unrolled thin mats and slept on the floor. Privacy did not exist; our lives unfolded in the single room, where every breath and silence was shared.

Outside, the reality of city life tested us each day.

A row of shared washrooms lined the narrow lane. The air was thick with a smell that never left.

My mother used to fetch water from a common pump, waiting in line with neighbors. She used to carry pots balancing on her waist, feeling drained when she returned.

Some mornings, we had to rush to the tanker, jostling for our share of water. Every drop came with a struggle, and every meal came with an effort.

And somewhere in that struggle, a quiet desire began to grow.

One morning, amidst the hustle, my mother held my hand and softly said, "Today, we'll visit your residential school."

I didn't know what to expect. To my surprise, my grandmother joined us, along with my uncle. Their presence motivated me on my first day.

We walked through the gates of Darulshifa Blind Boys' High School. The space buzzed with children's voices. Some laughed, called out to one another, and recited rhymes. Some were tapping teachers' canes on the ground, some reciting lessons, their voices carrying joy.

I clung to my mother's saree, unsure if I belonged here.

Both my mother and grandmother gently nudged me to step into the principal's office. Inside, there were two men talking. The principal and a teacher. Their voices carried warmth. I greeted both.

The teacher placed a few coins in my hand and asked, "Can you tell me what these are?"

I touched them, turned them over, and felt their weight and ridges. "Two rupees.. One rupee.. Fifty paise.." I answered, hesitant at first, then with growing confidence.

A murmur of approval followed. I had unknowingly passed an invisible test of touch and recognition.

The first few days were filled with mixed emotions. Curiosity, nervousness, and fascination. Needless to say, I was enjoying learning new things.

One of my first lessons was a rhyme, Chitti Chilakamma. A song about a little parrot. Initially, I was just listening to other children. Their voices rose in chorus, bright and cheerful. Eventually, I joined.

A few days later, while wandering down a corridor, I followed a melodious tone that took me to the music room.

Inside, Rama Rao Sir, who was blind himself, played the harmonium. I sat along with a bunch of students. He introduced us to basic ragas. I tried following his voice but trembled. I still tried to follow. I sang but didn't master the notes. But a feeling touched my heart that said I might belong here.

It was around this time that I was first introduced to Braille. The raised dots felt strange under my fingertips. Like a secret code meant for people like me. I started to move too fast but missed the patterns. Then I slowed down and traced each dot gently. It was like the world had opened a new door for me.

While I was adjusting to school life, my uncle believed I would also adapt to the hostel, where I was surrounded by other blind children.

The idea sounded simple, but the first day told a different story.

The hostel felt unfamiliar. I was outside my comfort zone. Thankfully, they allowed my grandmother to stay with me for a few days until I settled in.

There were no special dormitories for younger children. In those days, the same spaces were used for many purposes. One large hall functioned as a dining area for lunch and dinner, and at night it became a sleeping hall.

Most of us slept directly on the floor. There were no mattresses. Only thin mats spread side by side. Along one side of the same hall, huge wooden and metal containers stored hot food.

We were given small wooden boxes to keep our belongings. Those boxes were kept in a small room nearby, which often became hot from the stored food. Sometimes, we had to wait outside until everyone had finished dinner before we could go back inside.

It wasn't cruelty. It was simply how things were around 30 years ago. Education was not comfortable, and space was not sufficient. What mattered was that learning was happening, despite the hardship.

At night, children lay shoulder to shoulder on the hard floor, whispering and giggling before sleep. From the edge of a table, my grandmother tried to make space to rest. I slept on the floor, feeling the ground.

The next morning brought harsh realities. The toilets reeked, the stench was unbearable, and the floors were slick and buzzed with flies. Each sound and smell etched deep in my memory.

Days passed slowly; my grandmother tried to stay strong for me, but I could sense her struggle.

Though I kept quiet, not wanting to lose my chance to study, she could no longer bear it. She told my mother about the situation.

Not long after, my mother decided I wouldn't stay in the hostel. She came one morning, packed my stuff, held my hand, and took me home.

I was silent, thinking she wanted me to stop studying. But she told me that nobody could stop me from moving forward in life.

The next morning, she placed a handicapped bus pass in my hand. From that day onward, she would walk me to the bus stop, help me board, and travel with me to school. She waited outside the school until I finished my classes, and then we returned home together.

I enjoyed the bus rides with her, the jingle of coins, the conductor's whistle, and the rumble of the old engine. All of which became my daily melody.

The bus pass was not just a piece of paper for me; it was a lifeline and a bridge between me and my education.

Over time, we were becoming familiar with teachers and school staff. Some, but not all, teachers were blind. My mother too had begun forming connections with people around the school. And one such connection was with Anasurya teacher, who was blind too.

The first time my mother met her, a bond formed instantly; these two women understood struggle without words. By a twist of fate, she moved into the house next to ours. From then on, she became more than a teacher. She was a family.

Every morning, the three of us walked together to the bus stop and then boarded a bus to school. There was something about that little procession. One blind woman, a small blind boy, and a sighted mother. That made people stop and stare.

Some looked puzzled, some whispered, and some offered help before we even asked. For strangers it was curiosity; for us it was comfort.

Anasurya teacher taught my mother how to navigate the city, how to buy from shops, and even how to eat food outside without hesitation. She showed my mother small, practical tricks like where the shopkeeper always kept the best rice, which bus conductor would be patient, and which lane had an easier step.

Her help was beyond skills. She was a steady advocate. She knew which doctor to visit when the need arose, she helped us learn Braille, and sometimes she simply sat with us and let silence do the healing.

People would sometimes whisper about the sight of us supporting one another as if dependence were a fault. But they didn't know that this dependence came from practice, pride, and refusal to be diminished.

To my mother, she was a map and a confidante; to me, she was a second mother who taught me small acts of dignity.

My mother leaned on her, and I, in turn, leaned on them both. With her by our side, the world began to feel a little less frightening.

But hardships still shadowed us.

I often played with a cycle tire, rolling it down the street with a stick, laughing as it clattered over stones. That sound was my delight.

One afternoon, I left it at the door while I went to the washroom. When I returned, I heard my mother crying. My father, drunk and angry, had used the same tire to hit her.

The sound of that tire, once my source of laughter, now froze my heart. I abandoned it that day. And with it, a piece of my childhood.

Months passed, nearly the end of my first standard, when life tested us again. My mother, pregnant with my sister, fainted on the road while on her way to pick me up. A lorry screeched to a halt, missing her by inches. Strangers rushed to her aid and carried her home.

That day, I waited at school for hours, not knowing what to do, tears rolling down my face with every passing minute.

Two senior blind boys heard me crying and asked about the situation. I explained them.

"Don't cry, come, we'll take you," one said gently, holding my hand. They guided me to the bus, paid my fare, and brought me home safely.

In the rush to reach my mother, I forgot to thank them. On the other side, I was glad that my mother was safe.

The next morning, I shared this incident with Anasurya teacher. She listened to me and said, "Nagababu, it's your duty to thank those who help you."

Her words stayed with me forever.

After my exams in April 1993, a fierce fight between my parents broke out at home.
My uncle got to know and arrived without warning. He took my mother, my younger sister Shailaja, and me to the bus station.

I remember the bus station's canteen clearly, the smell of sambar rice, a South Indian dish made of rice, vegetables, lentils, tamarind, and spices. The scent mixed with diesel fumes and the sound of bus horns. We ate quickly and boarded the bus.

The ride was long. Dust blew through the open windows, touching my face. Then came sudden rain; hailstones rattled against the roof of the bus. My mother, tired but alert, told me how rare such storms were.

That was my first memory of hail, the strange wonder of stones falling from the sky.

In July 1993, my second sister, Shanti, was born, tiny, fragile, and beautiful. But our joy soon turned to worry when the doctor said she too was blind.

My grandmother wept, holding the baby close and murmuring prayers. Even at that young age, I felt the heaviness in my heart.

A month later, my father came to Vuyyuru and took us back to Hyderabad. Soon after, my baby sister was admitted to Sarojini Devi Eye Hospital.

For seven long months, my mother stayed there, sleeping on the floor, living on meager meals, and whispering prayers. Her world had shrunk to that hospital ward.

Hope lingered in those sterile corridors like a fragile light.

When a donor eye was found for a corneal transplant, it felt like a miracle. We waited through sleepless nights of prayers, believing they might finally be heard.

But fate was not ready to change.

Our hope broke. The transplant failed.

During this period, I used to stay at the hostel and visit my mother and sister at the hospital on weekends. Thereafter, I continued to live in the hostel throughout my schooling.

I slept in the dining hall of the hostel, restless through the nights. Children snored nearby, rats scurried in the dark, and there was a lingering smell of cooked rice and lentil soup. Nights were long, but somewhere I began to find my flow.

Staying in the hostel, I learned to do all my daily chores as a normal person would do. I washed clothes, cleaned and organized my space, brushed and showered, and even helped my hostel mates.

During school holidays, leaving the hostel was easy, but coming back was not. I used to cry endlessly when it was time to return. The idea of being away from my mother and home broke me every single time.

But neither my mother, father, grandmother, nor other family members allowed that fear to weaken me. Sometimes, my father would cycle for 8 kilometers just to pick me up and drop me off at school and bring me back home. They spoke to me gently, sometimes firmly, always lovingly.

"Study," my mother would say. "This is your strength," my uncle reminded me.

Their belief was unshakable. They never treated my education as optional. They carried one clear intention in their hearts: that I must learn, that I must rise.

I often think that if I had not studied, I would not be here writing these words today. Their vision for my future became the map for my life.

At Darulshifa school, during those early days when everything felt unfamiliar and home seemed painfully far, I found comfort in a senior named Govind Reddy. He was a year older than me, gentle, calm, and understanding. The kind of friend who didn't need many words to make you feel seen.

We both carried the same ache of separation, the same quiet homesickness that comes from leaving one's parents too soon. In the silence of those hostel nights, when footsteps faded and thoughts grew louder, it was often Govind who helped turn loneliness into laughter.

We shared stories of our families, festivals we missed, and the small things we longed for. Like the smell of home-cooked food and the comfort of familiar voices.

In those moments, he was more than a senior; he was like an elder brother, guiding me through emotions I didn't yet know how to name. We studied together, played together, and learned to find joy in small things. From shared snacks to our walks across the school ground.

Even now, after so many years, Govind Reddy remains the same good friend in my life. Whenever I reach out to him, he is ready to listen and always encouraging.

That bond, built in the quiet halls of Darulshifa, has never disappeared. A reminder that sometimes life brings the right people to walk beside us long before we realize how much we will need them.

In the hostel, we invented our own games with whatever we had.

A coconut oil bottle filled with stones became our cricket ball, and a wooden slate became the bat. The rattle of the bottle guided us, and we chased it with joy.

For a while, all our worries disappeared.

By 1994, I was eight years old.

In two years, I had lived through more than I could understand: leaving my grandparents' home, discovering school, witnessing my sister's birth, traveling through storms, and learning that love sometimes meant endurance.

I wasn't just learning rhymes or alphabets. I was learning to survive and to find light even where there was none.

Education had begun for me, but so had life's hardest lessons.

Chapter 3: The colors faded, but dreams deepened

I was in my 3rd standard when I began noticing something strange about my sight. Until then, I could recognize colors faintly. Red, yellow, green. Though never with clarity.

One day, everything began to change. The world around me seemed to shrink into a single hue. Everywhere I turned, all I saw was red. It was as if someone had spilled paint across the canvas of my life and taken away every other shade.

At first, I thought it was temporary. Perhaps the sun was too bright or my eyes were tired. But the redness remained. Day after day, everything I looked at glowed in just one color. Fading, flickering, and blurring.

Fear crept in quietly, though I did not have words to describe it.

My mother noticed first. She saw the blood oozing from my nose and my eyes turning red. She always observed me. Every minute change. Every silent discomfort. Her eyes, though weary from years of adversities, never missed the smallest detail about me.

She held my face gently, asking questions I couldn’t answer. And as always, she gathered her courage and took me to Sarojini Devi Eye Hospital.

The doctor prescribed medications for a few days. But they did not provide any relief. My right eye began to burn.

We returned to the hospital. The doctor shone light into my eyes to examine them. In a low voice, he told my mother that my right eye was not responding. It was her worst fear. He further added that it must be removed; otherwise, it might harm me.

I heard those words but did not understand what "removal" meant. To me, the word sounded like misplacing a toy, taking something away, and keeping it aside for later. While I was trying to figure it out, I heard my mother’s soft sobs that carried the weight of helplessness.

She agreed to the surgery. She prepared me. But nothing could have prepared me for what came next.

The day of surgery arrived. The operating theater was cold, metallic, and unfamiliar. Strange voices floated above me, machines thrummed, and then everything slipped into darkness under anesthesia.

When I woke, the pain was unbearable. The right side of my face burned even more. A bandage pressed against my eye socket, pain throbbing with every heartbeat.

I held my mother's hand and cried. "Amma, it hurts!"

She stroked my hair with shuddering hands and whispered again and again, "It will pass, Nani.. it will pass."

That's the name she used lovingly for me.

But the pain didn't subside. It throbbed through the days and nights that followed. Every blink, every turn of my head, and every attempt to sleep brought fresh agony. Even today, the memory of it sends shivers through me.

Recovery was slow. Even painkillers barely helped.

I grew used to the bandage, to the hollow where my eye had once been. Yet something inside me changed.

Until then, for 8 years, I thought blindness was the absence of light. A condition I was born with.

Now I understood loss; it is the experience of having something and then having it taken away. Even as I slowly adjusted to life without sight, the world seemed reluctant to spare me.

In the same year, chickenpox swept through our family. First me, and then my sisters. Fever gripped us, burning like fire. Blisters erupted, itching unbearably, as if thousands of needles pricked at once.

My mother sat beside me, fanning me, applying neem paste to cool the rashes. And singing soft lullabies even when her own body ached.

While all of us were yet to recover, my father, drunk and angry, insisted we leave immediately for Jijivaram, his hometown.

In the middle of illness, we boarded the bus. I still remember that humid night, my body burning with fever, my sisters whimpering beside me, and my mother holding us close as the bus moved down the dark road.

I couldn't understand why we had to travel when we were so sick. I felt the storm of my father's anger and the unshakable shield of my mother's arm protecting us all.

Those nights left scars that no one could see, yet they remained. I was still a child, but I had already learned to live with pain, sudden displacements, and uncertainties of tomorrow.

While my parents and sisters stayed in Jijivaram, I was sent back to my hostel in Hyderabad. Life oscillated between hardships and small joys.

The nights were long and uneasy, filled with sounds that reminded us we were far from home, yet laughter still found its way into our days.

Every fortnight, Rajini aunty and her daughter Sowmya visited me. Sometimes my grandmother too came, with Sowmya. Their visits were the moments of light, filling the hostel with warmth.

Even my father visited occasionally, showing care in small ways. I started learning that people could hold feelings of love and fury in their same heart.

Cricket became my favorite escape. A plastic bottle served as a ball and the wooden slate as a bat. The sound of children laughing echoed louder than our struggles.

By 4th standard, I discovered a fascination for sound. Radios become my secret world. I even had one of my own, a tiny companion that spoke in rhythms and voices beyond sight. I listened to cricket commentaries, to voices rising and falling in excitement and tension.

During one unforgettable match between India and Pakistan, the commentator cried out in disbelief, "Anil Kumble had taken all 10 wickets in a single inning."

My body tingled with excitement. In those moments, blindness did not matter. I imagined the game in my mind clearer than sight could have provided me.

Sometimes, I opened the radio, tracing its circuits with my fingers as if reading the hidden map. I was curious to know how wires and switches produce voices. The curiosity stayed with me, a spark that would guide my future.

There came another day that left a deep, unspoken mark in my life.

My younger maternal aunt, Anuradha, held a special place in our hearts. She was affectionate and playful. And always took good care of my younger sisters and me.

In June 1996, on my birthday, she asked my mother to take her to the temple. My mother was busy with chores, so my aunt went alone.

The next morning, news struck like thunder. She and the man she loved, Srinu, had taken their own lives, afraid their families would disapprove of their marriage.

I was too young to grasp the situation, but I knew something irreparable had happened.

My grandmother's wails filled the house. My mother was speechless. And I wondered silently, if Amma had taken her to the temple, would things have been different?

That tragedy taught me early what many learn late. That love can be crushed by fear. The family honor can weigh heavier than life itself. Every moment with those we love is precious.

That incident shaped how I valued relationships for the rest of my life.

By the end of that year, I was no longer the timid boy who once feared the sound of cinema halls. I had endured pain, be it emotional or physical. Yet, I found joy in the games and voices that spoke to me through radios.

The colors had faded from my world. My right eye was gone, and even the faint shades of red vanished. But I somehow had a different vision, the one made of sound, imagination, and resilience.

That was when I began to understand. Blindness might take away the light, but never my dreams.

Chapter 4: The turning point

The years I spent at Darulshifa gave me the first taste of education. Those lines shaped my childhood with challenges I couldn't yet name.

I still remember sleeping in the dining hall, the smell of sambar or vegetable lentil soup lingering long after dinner, and rats scurrying across the floor while we curled up on thin mats.

Through those years, Anasurya teacher stood beside my mother like family. Her steady hand in our long struggle gave us enough strength to move on in life.

As school started to become my refuge, home was shadowed by another battle.

My parents were worried about the thought of sending me and my sister to two different schools because Darulshifa government school was only for boys.

Anasurya teacher saw my parents' struggle and the limited scope of continuing my studies in the Telugu medium at Darulshifa. She urged my parents to try for Devnar School for the Blind, a place she described as disciplined, visionary, and built to nurture children like us.

Even my parents believed that studying in the same school would strengthen our bond. And that we could lean on each other through every challenge.

Devnar School for the Blind was founded by the renowned ophthalmologist and visionary Dr. Saibaba Goud. He offered what no other school could. Free, high-quality education, an English-medium curriculum, structured learning, and a belief that blindness was not a barrier but a beginning.

Above all, the possibility for my sister and me to study together became the only path forward.

The day we entered Devnar felt less like a transfer and more like a destiny taking shape. My mother held our hands as we climbed the steps, her grip loosening slightly.

The building loomed ahead, bright and strange, yet welcoming. There was no chalk scratching on the blackboards, corridors buzzed with energy, the tip-tap of styluses punching Braille dots, teachers dictating lessons, and children whispering in Braille.

From nearby came the clatter of Taylor's frames, the pins sliding quickly as students solved problems. And as always, drifting in from the kitchen was the smell of steaming rice and lentil soup, mingling with children's chatter.

That morning I held my sister's hand tightly. We were both uncertain of what awaited us. But we were together in this new world, and that steadied my heart.

I also felt something new here. That blindness was not a boundary; it was just another way of learning.

Excitement soon gave way to reality.

Here, every subject was taught in English. I tried to cope, but words slipped through my grasp.

I did not realize how the days were passing. And then came the day of my first unit test. It was a social studies paper. My fingers traced the Braille dots, but they seemed foreign. Line after line I struggled, unable to understand. But I tried to give my best.

After a few days, the results were out. Shravanthi Madam called out, "Nagababu… one mark."

A few children chuckled, and whispers spread across the class. Until then, I had considered myself bright. But I felt humiliated.

That evening, I refused to have food and sat on my hostel mat. For the first time, I wondered if my relatives in Vuyyuru were right. Maybe blindness truly meant education was not for me.

Days passed like that. I went to class, but the joy I had once in learning had dimmed. I listened more than I spoke. Every mistake felt bigger than the last.

It was one of those dull days that the school hosted a dental camp. While I was outside the classroom waiting for my turn at the camp, Shravanthi Madam told my class, “Don’t laugh at Nagababu. Yes, his marks are low today, but he is improving. And as he continues, he will rise.”

I wasn’t there to hear it myself. I only learned what she had said when a classmate whispered it to me later. At first, I thought he was teasing me. But then another classmate confirmed it. And then another.

Her one sentence changed something inside me. “He will rise.”

She didn't speak of possibility; she spoke of certainty.

Shravanthi Madam was strict and disciplined, the kind of teacher who expected effort from everyone. But behind her firmness was her deep compassion. She noticed our struggles but refused to let any of us fall behind.

She recorded our lessons, like every other teacher did, on audio cassettes. However, she put in an extra effort by recording subjects other than hers. She made us believe that if the world tried to limit us, learning would set us free.

Her faith became my light. Perhaps small from the outside, but to a boy drowning in doubt, it was everything.

For most children, learning happens through sight. Letters on blackboards, numbers in chalk, and diagrams sketched in white strokes. For me, learning was a matter of sound, touch, and patience. Everything had to pass through my fingertips before it reached my mind.

The Taylor's frame became my first companion in mathematics. Though I was familiar with it, I doubted if I would ever feel capable of using it.

Taylor's frame is a simple wooden tool with metal grooves and tiny movable pins. Yet for a blind student, it was a complete mathematical universe.

Each groove meant a place value. Units, tens, and hundreds. Each pin flipped or moved became a number or sign. Addition, subtraction, multiplication. Everything can be done silently by the feel and the click of the pins marking every step.

Around this time, Rajashekhar Sir entered my learning journey. Firm in voice yet encouraging in nature, he always told us to think and not just repeat.

He gave us a sum to solve one day. My fingers moved quickly, counting, aligning, and calculating. I read out the answer while my heart was pounding.

A breath of silence. Then his voice rang, "Correct. Absolutely correct!"

That praise didn't just acknowledge my right answer; it restored confidence that one mark in social studies had broken.

It was during my quarterly examinations that I gained confidence by solving a number of problems. I realized that I could do well and be at par with other students.

Over time, the frame became a language of logic. When the pins aligned perfectly, I felt a pride that others found in neat handwriting.

Alongside Taylor's frame, I used to write with the Braille slate and stylus. They were my first writing tools. Dots embossed from the back made every letter mirror-reversed. I wrote from right to left so I could read later from left to right. Tap… tap… tap.. The stylus on thick paper became the sound of my independence.

Every note, every test, and every dream began as small raised dots under my fingertips.

Together, the Taylor's frame and Braille slate taught me discipline, structure, and courage. And showed me that blindness wasn't a barrier to knowledge. It was only a different path.

Not long after, two new teachers entered my life who shaped me forever, Mr. Egbert Dawson and Mrs. Lilly Egbert. They were a retired couple with decades of experience with pure love for teaching.

Egbert Sir taught Biology; Lilly Madam taught English and Mathematics. They spoke only in English, which terrified me at first. But listening to them and responding in hesitant sentences built my confidence more than any textbook could.

Lilly Madam was calm. But her patience was extraordinary. “Read again,” she would say gently. “Don’t be afraid of mistakes.”

Her voice carried no frustration, only faith. Her gentle encouragement built my confidence in English and Mathematics. And slowly, my fear for English began to fade, which later became essential in my professional life.

Egbert Sir, on the other hand, had a different energy. Firm but full of enthusiasm. He wanted us not only to learn but also to truly understand. He treated blindness not as a limitation but as an invitation to teach differently. His creative experiments and explanations turned science into something I could feel and imagine, not just memorize.

One day, he announced a project about raised diagrams. “For blind students,” he said, “touch can replace sight.”

He assigned me the human blood circulation system. For days, I soaked paper until it softened, pulped it with my hands, and shaped it from paste. The smell of wet paper clung to me.

On a plywood board, I laid ropes to form veins and arteries, pressing the paste along them under his guidance. "Thicker here, curve there," he'd say, his voice full of excitement.

When it was done, I ran my fingers over it, and for the first time, I could feel the flow of blood.

At the science fair, I stood proudly before visitors from elite schools, explaining the project with confidence. Their surprise and admiration washed over me.

Then came a turning point that would shape my future, the computer. My first computer lessons came from Kavitha Madam, who introduced me to MS-DOS. Commands like cd, dir, and copy felt like spells that summoned action.

With the JAWS screen reader, the machine spoke back to me.

Later, Sudha Madam deepened my learning.

Computers didn't judge blindness; they simply responded. I felt free, a kind of independence no limitation could cage.

Among many friendships I formed at Devnar, two hold a special place in my heart, Pavan and Kalishekar.

They weren't in my batch. Pavan was two years junior, and Kalishekar was one year junior. But in spirit, we were equal. Inside those hostel walls, age meant nothing. What truly connected us was understanding, loyalty, and the quiet comfort of friendship.

We were inseparable. Three boys walking, laughing, and dreaming together.

If Pavan brought focus and fierce determination, Kalishekar brought calm and warmth. I was somewhere in between, often the listener, sometimes the orator. Together, we were a balance of energy, patience, and joy.

Pavan was not the kind who spoke much, but he was always there. When situations grew complicated, his presence became a quiet assurance. He didn't ask what I needed every time; he simply stayed close enough that I never felt alone.

Our happiest moments were simple, like washing clothes together near the hostel water tank and buying ice cream sticks outside the hostel gate.

We turned even those pure moments into memories. Buckets clanked, soap foamed, and our voices rose over the sound of running water. We teased each other, splashed playfully, and talked about everything. Our futures, our fears, our little victories.

To this day, the faint smell of soap and the sound of water take me back to those evenings when friendship made even the ordinary feel special.

We shared everything, whispered secrets after lights-out, had laughter that echoed down the corridors, and engaged in small mischiefs that only children could invent. Those moments weren't grand, but they built something that time couldn't erase.

Even now, years later, when we speak, it feels as if nothing has changed.

Three boys, still laughing somewhere inside the corridors of Devnar, walking side by side along an unseen path that has kept us connected forever.

At Devnar, not every lesson came from classrooms. Some of the most beautiful ones came from having fun. From giggles on the playground while playing with wooden bats and rattling balls to board games where fingers moved like thoughts.

The Devnar school ground echoed with laughter, calls, and the clatter of metal-filled balls. We played with official cricket kits for the blind. Real bats, stumps, and white cricket balls with small bearings that rattled when rolled or thrown.

First, the bowler says, 'ready.' Then the batsman responds. Then the bowler says, 'play' and releases the ball. Blind cricket has its own harmony. Cricket teams have three groups.

B1, totally blind; B2, partially blind; and B3, limited vision.

Each one plays a part that completes the whole.

Sighted team members on the boundary call out directions, "Ball left!" or "Run straight!"

It wasn't chaos. It was music. A field alive with voices and beliefs.

I never played official tournaments, but I played countless games on the Devnar ground.
We laughed. We fought playfully. And the rattling ball echoed like joy itself.

Those afternoons were about freedom, courage, and friendship.

Cricket taught me to listen. Listen to my teammates, to the ball, to life itself. It taught me that sometimes you don't need to see the direction. You just need to trust your instincts and swing.

If cricket was the sound of freedom, chess was the rhythm of thought.

For many, chess is a game of sight with black and white squares. Mapped and measured by the eyes. For me, it was a world we built through touch and memory.

Our boards were tactile. Black squares were raised slightly higher. Each piece had a tiny peg beneath it, fitting into holes on the board so they wouldn't topple. The black pieces had a small metal dot on top, a mark I could feel instantly.

Every move began with my fingertips, tracing the board and building the game's picture inside my mind.

In official tournaments, blind players use two boards: a tactile one for the visually impaired and a regular one for sighted opponents, kept in sync by the arbiter.

But in most of my games, both during school and later in college, I played directly on my tactile board with sighted players, simply announcing every move aloud. What started as curiosity in their eyes turned into respect once the game began.

Chess became my mirror, a way to measure my patience and focus. It made me feel equal, not through sympathy, but through intellect. Each move was a statement that my mind saw what my eyes couldn't.

Each game reminded me how far I've come. From those early Devnar classrooms to this life built on focus and faith. For me, chess was never about winning or losing. It was about patience, discipline, and clarity.

It was the art of thinking several moves ahead, even when I could not see the board.

Vision, I learned, isn't just sight. It's awareness. It's knowing where your next step should be.

Those hours on the cricket field and at the chessboard quietly shaped me. Every sound- and touch-trained move was a lesson in patience and faith.

Devnar wasn't only teaching me to play. It was preparing me for life's bigger tournaments. The ones that test not your skill but your spirit. The test came sooner than I expected. The South Zone Chess Tournament for the Blind. For me, it was more than a game. It was a chance to prove myself.

My father bought me my first pair of jeans. To me, it meant everything, a rare luxury. It made me feel grown up, confident, and ready.

In the first match, I whispered a quiet prayer before my move, and I won. In the next, I prayed again, and I won again.

Confidence grew, quietly but steadily.

But as the games continued, I began to believe I no longer needed help. I was careless. I stopped praying. And then came the losses. One, then another, and then another.

By the 5th loss, I could no longer hold back. Tears fell on the board I had once traced with pride.

That was when my teacher, Dilip Reddy Sir, and my coach, Chandrashekhar Sir, came to me. They placed their hands on my shoulders and said gently, "Nagababu, don't cry. Winning and losing are both part of life. Learn from this."

Their words sank deep. In the games I prayed, I had played with humility. In the ones I didn't, I played with pride.

That lesson has stayed with me: faith and devotion must not be occasional. They should stay with you. Quiet, constant, and guiding you through every move in life.

That tournament didn't just test my chess skills. It revealed something about who I was becoming. A boy learning not only how to win but also how to lose with grace.

Devnar was not just a school, it was my stage. One that took me from shame to strength, from whispers of doubt to voices of encouragement, and from a young boy who thought he couldn't to a teenager who believed he could.

Chapter 5: Between questions and quiet bonds

By the time I reached 9th standard at Devnar, I was no longer the hesitant boy who had once scored a single mark in social studies. My foundation years of struggle, encouragement, and discovery had shaped me.

English was still a mountain, but now I could climb it. I began to debate in class and raise doubts with confidence. Somewhere along the way, I had found my voice.

It was during my high school years at Devnar that I met one of the most influential teachers in my life. Swarnalatha Madam. She taught civics, but what she truly imparted went far beyond law and constitution.

Her classes were alive with questions, laughter, and healthy arguments. She didn't want us to memorize, she wanted us to think. Her presence commanded both respect and warmth. She had a way of turning silence into curiosity, making even reluctant students speak.

By then, my questions had begun to stretch beyond textbooks. I found myself drawn to discussions on women's rights, dowry, social inequality, and fairness within society. These were the topics that I did not fully understand, but they troubled me deeply. At that age itself, I started to feel that dignity and equality should not be selective.

Every lesson began not with a definition, but a question. She asked one afternoon, "What is democracy?"

Voices around me rose. One boy said, "Government by the people," and another said, "Rule of the people."

It was my turn when my fingers rested on the Braille paper. I then said, "Madam, if democracy means equality, why are children like us still denied admission to schools and colleges? And why do women still have to fight for basic respect inside their homes?"

The room turned silent. Swarnalatha Madam chuckled and replied, "Nagababu,, you always turn my class into a debate. That's good, never stop questioning."

Her words echoed in me long after that day. In her class, I wasn't just another student memorizing lines. I was someone whose thoughts mattered. Through her lessons, I discovered that the right question could open more doors than the right answer.

Swarnalatha Madam was more than a teacher, she was a catalyst. She taught me that questioning was not rebellious; it was awareness. She encouraged me to speak, analyze, and challenge injustice. And more importantly, to believe that my words had power.

That belief shaped the person I became, one who could articulate his thoughts, defend his rights, and lead with conviction.

Later, during my ECET and engineering admissions, it was her husband's, Mr. Gunashekar's guidance, that became my anchor. His moral, intellectual, and financial support kept me moving when the path ahead seemed uncertain. He reminded me that equality is never granted, it must be earned with courage and persistence.

Together, Swarnalatha Madam and Mr. Gunashekar didn't just teach me lessons, they made me strong for the future. One gave me the courage to question, and the other gave me the strength to act. And both gave me a purpose that continues to guide me even today.

As I entered 10th standard, life tested me again. On the first morning of my board exams, I received a call at the hostel phone. It was from my father. His voice subdued, "Your grandfather is not well," he said. "We're going to the village."

I listened to him calmly and then walked into the exam hall. Those words still echo in my mind.

For the next several days, I wrote my papers, convincing myself he would recover. I imagined him waiting in our hometown and blessing me from afar.

After the last paper, we had a farewell party. Laughter, songs, and speeches about the future. I joined the party, pretending to feel the excitement of a boy who had completed school.

Only afterward, when my parents returned, did they tell me the truth. That my grandfather had passed away.

The moment I heard, the ground beneath me seemed to have collapsed. The man who had prayed for me, who had been a pillar of strength in my childhood, was gone. And I was not told. I hadn't been given the chance to mourn him. My parents hid the news so I could focus on my exams.

Though I understood them, the pain ran deep. It taught me that education sometimes demands sacrifices, even the chance to say goodbye.

Around this time, another episode unfolded in our family. One that shaped the direction of my life far more than I understood then.

My younger sister had been admitted to Devnar around the same time as me. The truth being, I was sent to Devnar because of her. My parents wanted both of us to study in a school that understood blindness. They felt she would need my presence, and I, in some way, went along as her companion.

But life often takes strange turns. I flourished in Devnar, and she couldn't.

She found hostel life overwhelming. She missed our mother deeply. The routine, the unfamiliar faces, the emotional distance, everything weighed heavily on her. When she matured, the school called my mother urgently. My mother rushed and took her to our hometown for some time.

Those days were filled with uncertainty, my mother torn between caring for her daughter and keeping my education moving.

However, she completed her intermediate, which is 11th and 12th standard, at Royal Junior College.

She soon stepped into the next phase of her life. Marriage, responsibilities, and a quieter path.

But, even today, a truth lives inside me like a small, silent weight. I rose because of her. I could move forward but she could not. And I regret that till this day. She was a part of my turning points and in every milestone I achieved. But I couldn't help her much when she needed me.

Some victories are bright, others carry shadows. Hers is the shadow that shaped my light.

When my 10th standard board exams ended in March 2002, there was almost a month between the results and the next step. That waiting period was longer than the exams.

In those days, results did not arrive with a click or a notification. The internet was raw, unreliable, and even expensive. There were no smartphones, no Wi-Fi accessible in homes, and cyber cafes charged by the minute for painfully slow speed. Most families didn't even consider checking results online.

The real announcement came through newspapers.

On the result day, people lined up early at newspaper shops, scanning long columns of hall ticket numbers printed in small size. Passing meant finding your number there. And the absence meant failure. It was a quiet, public reckoning.

Before stepping into that moment, I did something unexpected.

During my board exams, the scribe assigned to me was Jayalakshmi. She was a 9th standard student from another school. She had been patient, clear, and kind. At the end of the exams, she had handed me a piece of paper with her phone number, saying, “If you ever need help, you can call.”

That morning, before checking the newspaper, I dialed her number from a nearby public phone. “Hello, Jayalakshmi, this is Nagababu.”

There was a brief pause, and then her voice brightened. “Congratulations,” she said warmly.

I froze. “For what?” I asked, genuinely confused.

“You’ve passed,” she answered, smiling through her words. “I saw your result in the newspaper.”

For a moment, I couldn’t speak. I hadn’t seen the result yet. I didn’t know my marks. But the certainty in her voice made me feel lighter and fuller.

When I finally checked, my family gathered around. I had scored 68.16%

Relief entered the room, followed by questions that always come next. “What now?”

Some relatives suggested Law. "It will suit you," they said. "You have a strong memory, you can argue cases, and you will earn respect."

Others advised me to choose something safe, maybe a government job as a typist or a telephone operator.

But deep inside, I already knew the answer.

During this time, my father did something that changed my life further.

He bought me a computer. It was the year 2002, and for most families like ours, a computer was a rare and expensive thing. I still remember the soft sound of that new machine in our small home, a sound that felt like the future calling.

This is when one of my freelance teachers, Prasad, began visiting us every day. He too was blind, but he was skilled with screen readers and typing. Patiently, he guided me through the basics on how to use JAWS, how to navigate folders, and how to listen to a computer. In those days, I worked mostly with the demo version of JAWS, which forced me to restart the system every 40 minutes. That limitation stayed with me until my first corporate job. Yet, with those interruptions, those daily lessons opened a new world of confidence.

Ever since my first computer class at Devnar School, I've heard the voice of the screen reader, JAWS, reading commands aloud. I got to know where I belonged.

The click of the keyboard felt like music. Computers spoke a language I understood. They followed logic, not sight. They demanded focus, not sympathy.

So when people asked, “Law or Engineering?” I smiled quietly.

Engineering. Computers. That is my path.

However, I knew that passion alone was not enough.

To enter engineering, I had to clear the Polytechnic entrance exam. But finding accessible material was almost impossible. This is where Pavan's help became priceless once again. He remained a constant. Even when words failed me, knowing he was nearby made the uncertainty easier to carry. His neighbor in Vuyyuru owned old study books. And he shared them with me.

During holidays, a girl from our street read them aloud while I listened, memorized, and practiced.

Some nights the syllabus felt endless. But I repeated the same words to myself, "You will rise." Those were Shravanthi madam's words, and they became my lifelong mantra.

By then, hostel life had changed for me. I was no longer the frightened boy adjusting to dining hall floors and strange-smelling washrooms.

I was a senior now.

Younger students came to me for help with Braille or guidance about studies. I shared food, comforted them, and became the elder brother I once wished for.

We celebrated every festival with pride.

On Independence Day, our voices rose with patriotic songs.

On Louis Braille's birthday, we gave speeches honoring the man who had lit our path.

For me, standing and speaking before others was a victory in itself. Proof that I had come far from the silent child I once was. At night, the hostel buzzed with laughter and whispers, but before I slept, I often thought of the road ahead.

Childhood was ending.

Before me stretched a battlefield. Polytechnic, engineering, and a world that would test me harder than ever. But I was ready.

Chapter 6: The wall I had to break

During April and May 2002, while preparing for the Polytechnic entrance exam, I also applied for commerce seats in several Hyderabad colleges. This was just a backup plan. Something to fall back on if Polytechnic didn't work out.

Those visits revealed another truth. One that stung more than failed exams could. Most colleges refused to take my application. Even the high-ranking officials were reluctant to offer me a chance.

Their words were all the same. "Blind students are not eligible for Commerce." "They usually join H.E.C." History, Economics, Civics.

"C.E.C is difficult, we cannot take responsibility." C.E.C is Civics, Economics, Commerce.

"Come with a parent, and we will see." "We don't have facilities for you."

Some didn't even bother to give reasons; they said no. A few allowed to submit forms only when I insisted. I literally placed the applications on their desks and refused to walk away until they accepted.

But when merit lists were announced, my name was missing every single time. The college had never intended to include me.

Still, the sting never turned into doubt. Those applications were just fallbacks. My real fight, my dream, was Polytechnic.

One summer evening, our entire hope narrowed into a single booklet. My mother sat under a dim, flickering yellow bulb and read the Polytechnic prospectus aloud.

She read slowly and carefully because she knew how much every word meant to me. My father leaned against the wall listening. She hesitated reading, “Candidates with more than 40% disability are not eligible to apply.”

She went still. Even the noise from outside faded. She said softly, “Nani.. you are 100% blind.”

For a moment, nobody moved. My mother clutched my hand tighter as if hoping the rule would change if she held me. But instead of breaking me, something inside solidified. “I will still apply,” I said quietly. “Let them stop me if they can.”

I went ahead and applied. Not out of rebellion, but because the rule itself felt like a wall built without understanding. A wall meant to be broken.

But the real test arrived on the day of the exam. While I hoped they would give me a scribe who could read well and help me navigate the paper, I experienced the opposite.

I remember the exam was in the last week of April. The hall smelled of fresh ink and dust, and my heart felt like it was running a race inside my chest. I was assigned one scribe who was from the Telugu-medium background. She struggled to read the questions.

Every question became a puzzle I was trying to decode. Her pauses, her confusion, her mispronunciations. They all added layers of difficulty I had not prepared for.

The Polytechnic exam was bilingual, in English and Telugu. Since I could understand Telugu, I told her to continue reading in Telugu, even if it was slow.

But the damage was done. The exam felt like running a race with a twisted ankle. And I knew, deep inside, that my performance had taken a hit.

A few weeks later, in May, the results came. I got 52,217 rank. Qualified. It was not the best rank. It was not the worst. It was enough, I thought. I knew it was not because of lack of preparation but lack of accessibility.

It was my counseling day, 1st June 2002. It is a day for the official admission process once you get the rank. The qualified candidates are allotted seats in different diploma courses and colleges based on their rank, score, preference, and, of course, the availability of seats.

Before sunrise, my parents and I were ready and left for the counseling session. My father carried my documents like treasure, while my mother packed curd rice in a small steel box.

As we entered the counseling hall, it bustled with voices. And the ceiling fans barely moved the heat. I had no idea the hardest battle was just beginning.

When my turn came, the doctor scanned my file.

"100% blindness. Not eligible," she said flatly.

My father protested, "But he wrote the exam and secured a rank."

Another officer muttered, “Why waste time, Babu? Polytechnic is not for him. Try typewriting or telephonic work. Be practical.”

At 16, I could hear strangers already defining what I could or could not become. Their words hit me like knives.

My fists tightened. “I don’t need your advice,” I said louder than I meant, though shaking. The room fell silent, and we walked out without uttering another word.

While we were outside on the pavement, I felt the silence of my parents. I firmly yet quietly said, “We will go to the Commissioner for Disabled Welfare.”

My parents hesitated, but they followed. We took another bus right from where we were standing. It was another long ride through noise and heat.

We reached the Commissioner’s office, and it smelled of ink and paper. When the Commissioner for Disabled Welfare, Dr. R. Sundar Vadan, arrived, I explained everything. My heart was pounding, but my voice was steady.

He listened calmly as I said, “There is law, sir. The Equal Opportunities Act of 1995. No institution can deny education because of disability.”

The Commissioner accepted, wrote a letter, signed, and stamped it. “Take this to the counseling board,” he told us.

After a very long time, hope stirred. The next morning, we went to the counseling hall again. We showed the letter. The officials looked at it.

I was hoping for a positive answer. But I heard, “No.”

My father raised his voice, “This is from the Commissioner himself!”

Still they refused. We walked back through the crowd in silence, the heat pressing down, but something in me only grew harder.

That evening when everyone sat gloomy and depressed, I said, “We will go to the Commissioner of Technical Education.”

My parents, though not knowing what to do, supported me. The next morning, we took a bus and reached the office. The hall inside was large, filled with officials ringing telephones and clattering on keyboards.

After hours of waiting, the Commissioner of Technical Education, A. K. Sukumar, called us in. He read the letter carefully and said, “If this is the order, he must be given admission.”

Then, with a calm authority, he added that the college would ensure I received education and the right support.

Relief entered the room. My mother whispered a prayer, while my father exhaled a big sigh.

We were back at the counseling hall, this time confident. The officials who had dismissed us earlier were now silent, looking at the letter. They briefly exchanged murmurs and handed us the confirmation slip. On it was written, A. A. N. M. & V. V. R. S. R. Polytechnic, Gudlavalleru.

We left the hall with the slip, feeling lighter.

In fact, I felt taller with pride. My father’s voice was thick with emotion. He said, “It’s done.”

After several days of struggle, I had a wide smile on my face.

Chapter 7: When the walls turned into doors

My polytechnic journey didn't begin with a grand sense of victory.

It began quietly. Naveen had already become my compass whenever I was in Vuyyuru. He was my mother's brother's son. We had just two years of age difference. He was a brother I didn't ask for. He took me everywhere, to the fields, to the canals, to the small kirana shops or grocery stores, where the smell of jaggery sweets and savory snacks often attracted us. He never hesitated, simply caught my wrist and said, "Raa, Nani," which meant "Come, Nani."

Pavan, who also was from the same village, often joined us. Together, the three of us were noisy, carefree, and inseparable. We played cricket in the narrow lanes. Naveen batted and I bowled with all the seriousness in the world. I couldn't see the ball, but I heard its sound, the crack on the bat, and their screams. In those moments, I was not the blind boy that had to adjust. I was just another kid in the game.

And that's how we formed a strong bond at that age, which is still intact.

In a dawn-lit lane in Vuyyuru, often my grandmother's soft prayers drifting through the house and the familiar footsteps of my cousin Naveen calling out, "Nani! Come fast, we'll miss the bus!"

The air smelled of damp earth, wood smoke, and jasmine. Naveen's schoolbag bounced on his shoulder as he took my hand with a confidence far bigger than his age.

"Stone ahead… step right."
"There's water here… slow."
"Now straight."

He had memorized every crack and turn of the lane like a map etched in his mind. By the time we reached the Vuyyuru bus stand, the town had awoken.

Vendors selling hot idlis or steamed rice cakes, kettles whistling, and conductors calling destinations like drumbeats, "Gudivada! Machilipatnam! Vijayawada!"

Naveen guided me through the rush, settled me into the right bus, checked my bag twice, and whispered, "Don't worry, Nani. I told the conductor to stop at Gudivada."

The whistle blew. His voice faded as the bus moved forward. “Bye, Nani!”

Every turn, bump, and breeze soon became part of my internal compass. By the time we reached Gudivada, I stepped into another storm of sound. Hawkers selling fried snacks, rickshaw bells ringing, and students rushing.

There was no direct bus to Gudlavalleru. So every day I depended on kindness.

“I’m going to Gudlavalleru Polytechnic,” I would say.
And every day, someone replied, “Come, I’ll take you.”
“Hold my arm.”
“We’re going the same way.”

They helped me cross roads, spoke to conductors, walked me all the way to my classroom, made sure I reached safely, and then vanished into the crowd.

I learned kindness doesn’t have a face. It just becomes direction.

Gudlavalleru Polytechnic stood wide and welcoming. Long corridors that smelled of chalk, classrooms buzzing with chatter.

But what truly shaped my journey were the people.

At home, along with my mother, my uncle Venkateshwarao guided me on teenage challenges and imparted wisdom on values. Those lessons I still abide by.

Principal Ch. Venkataramanna wasn't just an administrator. He was the reason everything worked for me. Not only during college but also later in Hyderabad.

"Your success will be our pride, Nagababu," he once said. Those words stayed with me longer than any certificate.

The college management arranged scholarship and Ch. Venkataramanna Sir ensured I never lacked the tools to learn.

Shankar Rao Sir, the head of the department, was strict but fair. He would tap the desk and say, "No excuses. Explain the code." I wrote programs in Braille, line by line. He corrected my logic with patience, not pity.

Padhmaja teacher, who was a physics lecturer from Devnar, went beyond duty. During my first year in polytechnic, she drew tactile diagrams and sent them to me so I could feel and understand concepts others only saw. Those diagrams became my bridge to confidence.

Radha Madam, who taught Electrical Machines, did something extraordinary. She brought tactile diagrams into the classroom and often took extra time to help me feel and understand rotating fields, armatures, and machines that most people only learn visually. She never rushed me. Neither did she make me feel different.

Outside classrooms, chess became my quiet battlefield. I enjoyed it often in polytechnic, encouraged strongly by our sports Sir Sivaram, who believed competition sharpened confidence.

Once, I played a long, intense chess game against an engineering student who was a university-level finalist. The game stretched for nearly 3 hours. I don't even remember who won. What I remember is the silence around us. Everyone watching us in awe. That game taught me that attention is sometimes the loudest applause.

On the other hand, Sarojini Madam turned programming into poetry. "Nagababu," she would say, "now tell me what this loop does."

I visualized the flow, explained it, and her approving nod was worth more than grades.

A.V. R. Sir, the mathematics lecturer, used to tell me, "Feel numbers; they'll never betray you."

And K.V.R. Sir, the English lecturer, made me believe that voice itself is power.

"You speak with conviction. Keep using that strength."

All of them encouraged me in different ways. However, Polytechnic days were not just about academics.

During my final year, there were days I managed with only dinner. To reduce food bills, I sometimes skipped lunch and survived on a packet of biscuits bought by friends.

There were mornings when my grandmother had to borrow 35 rupees, just enough for my bus fare, so I could attend college.

Sometimes, growth isn't dramatic. It's just the ability to endure without falling apart.

In 2003, life shook us again. My younger sister, who was blind, fell from an open terrace.

The news came without warning, the way fear always does. We rushed her to the hospital, hearts pounding louder than our footsteps. I remember standing there, realizing I didn't even have 10 rupees in my pocket to call my father from a telephone booth.

The doctors spoke of surgery we couldn't afford. With no other choice, we shifted her to a government ward, carrying not just her but also our fear, our limits, and our helplessness.

She survived. But something inside me broke that day. Quietly. Permanently.

I learned then that strength isn't always loud. It doesn't announce itself. Sometimes, strength is simply staying present when everything inside you is collapsing.

That realization stayed with me as I continued walking forward.

Not because life had become easier. But because I had learned that endurance itself is a form of courage. And that lesson still carries me through the years ahead.

My life there was stitched together by friends.

On tiring days, I stayed in their tiny rented room with two floor mats, a kerosene stove, and a sky full of ambition. Nights were filled with laughter, debates, and dreams lit by candlelight when power failed.

They read diagrams aloud, explained circuits patiently, and made sure I never missed a lesson.

When classes ended early, either Ravi or Raja would bring their bicycle. They would make me sit on the frame and hold the handle while I pedaled slowly down the college road.

Those slow rides were freedom. Wind in my hair, laughter around me, blindness forgotten.

Among all my companions, Deepthi was the calmest. Her voice became my evening classroom.

She read chapters aloud, recorded lessons on cassettes, and revised with me before exams. “Shall I repeat that once more?” she would ask gently.

Her patience had no edge. It was steady, gentle, and unwavering. She shared her lunch when I had no food. Her help was not sympathy; it was solidarity.

If Deepthi was my voice for learning, Rajini Madam was my compass. She typed every note Deepthi wrote, turned them into computer files, and made sure I could access everything with my screen reader. Her kindness extended beyond the classroom.

Every evening, she walked with me from the college to the bus stop. “Careful, small step here… straight now… bus coming to the right.”

She held my hand, not out of fear that I would fall, but out of certainty that I must not walk alone.

At the Gudlavalleru bus stop, amid the noise of engines and chatter, she ensured I boarded safely.

On the bus, she talked about her mother’s cooking, old films, or the lessons of the day. Her voice drew a circle of tranquility around me.

At Gudivada, before parting, she insisted, “Let’s have something cool.”

We stood at a tiny cool-drink stall, sipping Fanta under the flickering tube light.
The sweetness of the drink, her laughter, the noise of the town. Those five minutes were my small celebrations of life.

Only after leading me to the Vuyyuru bus did she leave. She used to tell the conductor, “He’s my student. Please make sure he gets down safely.”

Before parting, she’d pat my shoulder, saying, “Now go home and eat something.” Her voice trailed behind the departing bus, “Good night!”

By the time I reached Vuyyuru, my grandmother used to wait for me at the bus stop. Even before stepping down, I would hear her soft call, “Come, Nani.”

Her hand found mine. Steady, warm, and eternal. From one caring hand to another, my day completed a full circle.

Those evenings taught me that kindness, given without expectation, becomes strength, and that strength carried me farther than any sight ever could.

My first year in Polytechnic was a year of learning, adjusting, and constantly proving that I deserved to be in the classroom. Everything was new for me as well as for the faculty and staff of the college. But they never left any stone unturned to support me.

Rural institutions in the early 2000s had not taught blind students. They did not have knowledge on how to guide me, but they provided me every support possible.

For instance, no technical subjects can be taught without diagrams. But for me, faculty always took an extra effort by drawing the diagrams on the tactile boards and giving them to me before the class began.

When exams arrived, I wrote every paper the way I knew. It was by preparing well and giving my best.

The testing method for visually impaired students was different. We had a scribe, usually a junior class student, who wrote for us. But for me, a nontechnical person was assigned as a scribe for polytechnic exams. So every diagram, formula, and circuit explanation had to be drawn roughly by me so they could replicate it on the answer sheet. Though they were unaware of the diagrams, they followed my scribbles to make a fair copy.

A single mistake in dictation meant a completely different answer on the paper.

Also, the State Board of Technical Education followed a strict process. My answer sheets were sealed and packed separately. They were sent for special scrutiny for evaluators to cross-check twice.

The college made sure of one thing: that no loose end was provided to me. They offered neither shortcuts nor special favors.

The day my results were out, I was shocked. I had cleared my theory papers, but practical exam marks were missing.

At first, I thought it was an error or a printing mistake. But then I was told that the management was not convinced of how a blind student could perform the practicals.

I paid visits to the State Board of Technical Education and spoke to the Commissioner and other officials. Principal Ch. Venkataramanna Sir also spoke to the officials and explained to them patiently about my situation through letters. He pushed to conduct things faster, to avoid delays that might affect my progression to the second year.

The board finally agreed to re-conduct the exam. During the re-exams, I performed every step slowly, describing each action and answering technical questions with clarity. There was no doubt left about what I knew.

Eventually, the marks came, and I had passed. That episode taught me that people may question your abilities, but they cannot override your perseverance.

By the final year, I wasn't just studying computers. I believed ideas could create change.

When the National ISTE Convention in Gujarat announced paper presentations, I submitted mine on "Empowering the Girl Child."

It came from my own experiences. My mother's courage, my sisters' struggles, the quiet battles of women around me.

The college management arranged sponsorship and Principal Ch. Venkataramanna Sir supported me well. He encouraged me, saying, "Go, Nagababu. The nation should hear your voice."

Rajini Madam refined my speech. Deepthi, along with other friends, helped me collect artifacts.

When I boarded the train with Rangababu Sir and other students, the smell of chai or tea, and the rhythmic clatter of train's wheels filled me with wonder.

At the venue, when I finally stood before a hall of professors in Gujarat, my hands shivered. But when I began to speak, fear slipped away. I spoke of dignity, opportunity, and the right of every girl to dream.

When I finished, silence held for a moment. Then applause rose like a storm. I had won first prize at the national level.

A girl from another college approached, placed a rose in my hand and said, "Your words inspired me."

I kept that rose pressed in my file for years. It was a reminder that truth, when spoken from the heart, can move mountains.

I rushed to the telephone booth to call and share the news with my family. But even before I could speak, I got the news, "Your mother is hospitalized."

My joy collapsed into worry. Life had a way of mixing the sweet and the bitter without warning. Whenever some happy moments arrived in my life, they were overshadowed with sadness. But I made sure that I maintained a balance between both situations.

Instead of panicking, I boarded a train to see my mother. When I finally saw her weak, lying on the hospital bed, I learned that success means nothing unless it's shared with those who carried you towards it.

Polytechnic life demanded endurance more than enthusiasm. On days when exhaustion crept in quietly, Pavan's presence reminded me that persistence did not have to be loud. It only has to be continuous.

When I look back, I do not remember the exhaustion, the two-bus commute, or the exams.
I remember hands that held mine, voices that guided me, and the hearts that refused to let me fall.

Those polytechnic days became the foundation of my life. I also attended campus selections held during that time. Unfortunately, the companies that interviewed me did not have suitable roles for me. But I did not lose my confidence. My faculty encouraged me to move on and go ahead with engineering so there would be broader opportunities for me.

Chapter 8: One voice against the rulebook

Some doors close quietly, while a few slam so loud that their echo follows you for years.

My journey toward ECET, the state-level Engineering Common Entrance Test, brought both kinds of doors into my path.

One day, during a free period in my polytechnic class, there were whispers between benches, under whirring fans, and with the faint scent of chalk. Someone mentioned, "Vedha Institute would soon start weekend sessions for polytechnic students." Another added, "Classes during long holidays might be given in Tanuku."

For most, ECET coaching was just another class. For me, it was a gateway to dignity, employment, and respect. A chance to rewrite destiny.

ECET was the only bridge for diploma students like us to enter into second-year engineering programs directly. Clearing it meant breaking free from the narrow lanes of limited opportunity and stepping into a world where technology and innovation waited.

Engineering was not just ambition. It was a world powered by computers, which had already lit a fire in me.

For a blind student, such dreams were rare. For me, they were necessary.

I enrolled in the classes without hesitation. On the first day of coaching, I sat in the front row, with a Braille slate, and my heart was racing. The room was warm, ceiling fans groaned under summer heat, and equations and technical concepts/algorithms rolled across the board like waves. I clung to every word.

During breaks, I stood outside with friends. Some shared a biscuit packet, and some recited formulas the way people sing movie songs. A breeze carried the smell of wet mud, the first sign of monsoon. In that very moment, I remember thinking. Maybe this storm is a sign for me.

The management of Vedha Institute waived my entire fee. Not out of sympathy, but belief. The director of the institute said softly, “Your effort is the best fee you can pay.”

Those words are still fresh in my memory.

The institute conducted longer sessions during long holidays in Tanuku, 125 kilometers from Gudlavalleru. The commute meant crowded buses and long hours. I remember the hustle, but I enjoyed every moment.

Each night when the world outside slept peacefully, my mind was always awake with formulas, algorithms, and hope.

My ECET exam was scheduled for 4 May 2005. Two days before the ECET exam, on the morning of 2 May, Naveen and I packed our bags and took a bus to Hyderabad. The city smelled of rain-soaked tar. The clouds were heavy, and puddles glimmered under streetlights. We stayed at Devnar School for the Blind. Familiar corridors and familiar warmth.

The same day, we went to the JNTU campus to check if the scribe is available for me on the exam day. The place buzzed with voices of nervous students, wet shoes squeaking on the wet tiles, and umbrellas dripping rainwater. I walked and walked to reach the room and handed the hall ticket to an officer.

He looked up sharply. "There's no scribe. You are not allowed to write the exam."

Again!

Silence crashed around me. My throat tightened. Not from fear, but fury this time. He returned my hall ticket and said, "Go home, babu. You can't take this exam."

I froze for a moment. I could do nothing. I turned and walked out. Each step felt heavier, but not weaker. If the system wanted to define my limits, I wanted to see how far it could go.

That night, around 8.30 p.m., back at Devnar, I called Swarnalatha Madam and explained the situation. Her voice carried the familiar blend of calmness and clarity. But this time, it had steel in it.

"We will not let this go," she said. "Come to my house at 6 a.m. tomorrow."

That night, sleep escaped me. I kept running my fingers over the hall ticket, feeling the embossed letters on its surface as if they carried my entire future.

The next morning, we started early and reached her home. Gunashekhar uncle took us in his car to the High Court. It was the first car journey of my life, but I couldn't experience the pleasure since I was all tensed.

By 11 a.m., Swarnalatha Madam and Gunashekhar uncle helped me file a petition in the Andhra Pradesh High Court. While we waited for the hearing, something clicked in him. He said, "Come, Nagababu, we are going to TV."

I had no idea what he meant.

He held my hand and led me to the TV9 news studio. There was light, sound, and hurried footsteps. Someone made me sit on a chair. I could feel cables beneath my feet. A microphone was clipped onto my shirt. A countdown began.

Gunashekhar uncle came to me and whispered, "Talk, Nagababu; tell them why you are fighting."

And the show started. I spoke a lot. About equality, ambition, and the right to dream. That day, millions heard the story of a blind student challenging the system that refused him a seat.

While I was being aired on the TV, the discussions related to me were happening at the High Court.

I did not know what was going to happen. Neither did I give any thoughts. I was rather thinking about how much Gunashekhar uncle and Swarnalatha Madam were helping me. Emotionally, financially, and morally.

He then dropped us at Devnar and I was waiting for the response. I called Gunashekhar uncle from the phone booth to inquire about the court's decision. And he responded, "Yes Nagababu. The court has directed the university to permit you to write the exam."

Mr. Gunashekhar and Swarnalatha Madam were not just happy for me but were proud.

After days and weeks of waiting and struggling, the ECET exam was just a day later. That night, I barely slept. Rain drummed on the roof, buses rumbled outside, and I rehearsed commands, formulas, and courage in my head.

On the 4th morning, Naveen, Gunashekhar Uncle, a junior lawyer, and a TV9 journalist accompanied me to the exam hall. The ground smelled earthy, and I was filled with anticipation.

A separate room was arranged for me. There was one desk, one chair, and for me, one chance. My scribe, provided by JNTU, was a nervous young man from a nontechnical background who sat beside me. He told me softly, “Let’s do our best.” His voice made me steady.

He read each question aloud, and I dictated answers, careful and calm. The scratch of his pen matched my heartbeat.

After the exam, when the bell rang, I leaned back, drained but grateful. I had written ECET, in defiance of a rulebook that had tried to erase me.

Outside, Naveen waited anxiously under a neem tree. He handed me a cup of tea. We stood in silence, sipping from hot steel tumblers. I was at utmost peace.

A few weeks passed. The summer was fading into monsoons. When results came, laughter filled college corridors. But my name was missing.

Results withheld.

Two words. I was crushed to the core.

Once again, Swarnalatha Madam stepped in. “This isn’t over,” she said.

She and Gunashekhar Uncle took me to the High Court. They told the judge; he frowned, tapped his pen, and ruled that JNTU must release Nagababu’s result.

On the day of counseling, my rank arrived. “State Rank 70.”

Sigh.

For someone who was told engineering is not for you, 70 was not just a rank. It was proof that persistence speaks louder than prejudice.

On the counseling day, my mother sat beside me. The official scanned my file and said flatly, “Blind students cannot be admitted.” The same wall, a different door.

My grip tightened on the desk. “I have fought too long for this,” I said. “I’m not leaving.”

After a few weeks, while Naveen, Pavan, and I were thinking about what to do, I called my friend Srinivas. Fortunately, he was in Hyderabad around that time. He was working for Manik Public School, Bangalore, then. I told him everything that was happening. He listened to me patiently and said, "We will fight this together."

True to his word, he joined me in every struggle that followed. He drafted letters, spoke to secretaries, and refused to let the file die on some dusty table. He wasn't there at the first spark, but when he came, he carried fire with him.

We travelled to the Secretariat and went to the Technical Education Commissioner to submit our pleadings.

Eventually, JNTU formed a special committee to decide if a blind student could really study engineering.

After a few months, I was called to JNTU and my mother accompanied me. A professor over there gave me a few lessons on computer operating systems, computer graphics, and computer networks and checked how I was comprehending. At that time, they had no JAWS screen reader.

Back then, I knew a JAWS vendor named Somaraj. I requested him to install a demo version in the university. Once it was done, I turned it on, and the screen reader's synthetic voice echoed the silent room. Then I reached for the breadboard, resistors, and wires. By touch alone, I assembled the circuit. Once the bulb glowed, there were whispers in the room.

One of the officials had asked me to execute a couple of programs to test my ability. The complete process took about 5 to 6 hours.

For a long moment, no one spoke. The room was silent, not out of doubt, but surprise. The kind that makes people pause because their assumptions have just been overturned.

Days later, a sealed envelope arrived. It felt heavier than paper, like justice arrived.

Inside was the Government Order, dated 7 October 2005. "Nagababu Jannu shall be admitted to Engineering."

This GO was given specifically mentioning my name. It was used as a reference for other students. Mostly everyone had to follow the same approach of testing. Even Pavan had to go through the same challenges I faced, from his Polytechnic admission to ECET counseling.

A special counselling session followed.

Gudlavalleru Engineering College opened its gates, not reluctantly but proudly.

The college management waived my fees, arranged accommodation, and provided a personal computer. Principal Ch. Venkataramanna Sir, my guardian, once again became my shield. He said, “You fought for this door to open, Nagababu. Now walk through with your head high.”

Soon, the story spread like wildfire. TV, newspapers, and magazines.

One of the journalists asked the chairman of the institution, V. V. R. Sheshadri Rao, “What motivated you to establish a college in a rural setting?” “Why are you supporting this boy who is going through many challenges already?”

He answered, “I did not have such a high level of education. That’s why I wanted every student to pursue their dreams irrespective of their background.”

During that time, reporter Sitaram, from Eenadu, one of the popular newspapers, was covering my progress. He played an instrumental role in getting my admission into engineering college. He wrote an article about me asking for sponsorships to support my education. A couple of people have approached to help me, but the college management supported me by then.

I remember one anonymous person from Hyderabad sending a money order of Rs. 5000 and wishing me good luck. I really cherished that moment. A stranger wrote my name and village name, and the way he appreciated me in his note was heart-touching. I also wrote back to him a couple of times expressing my gratitude.

JNTU refused to let me write exams. The reason they quoted was insufficient attendance. Though the delay had been theirs. Delayed admission because of systemic barriers.

I had to go to the court again. This time, the judge not only sighed but was half smiling and half weary. “You may continue,” he said, “but you must complete two semesters together.”

Two semesters. That was twice the syllabus, twice the pressure.

Some nights I studied till dawn, my fingers aching from typing Braille notes. Other nights, I fell asleep on the keyboard, dreaming of codes.

I told myself that if the world wanted to drown me, I would learn to breathe underwater.

Every morning I travelled by bus from Vuyyuru; dust, diesel, and determination became my companions. Some days I stayed with my cousin Soumya and other days with Pavan, who always made sure I never fell behind.

Deepthi, Vishalakshi, and other friends became my lifeline. They read lessons aloud, turned them into tapes, and even prepared tactile diagrams. Their voices became my textbooks, and their faith became my strength.

But support didn't come only from friends and classmates. It came quietly and consistently from people whose roles were never meant to be responsible for someone like me, yet whose humanity made the difference.

At Polytechnic, the departmental staff member, Peraiah, became one such pillar. On days when friends were unavailable, he would guide me through the campus, helping me navigate corridors, offices, and labs. Whenever I needed to visit the bank, nearly 1.5 kilometers away, he would seat me carefully on his bicycle and take me there. There was no obligation in his actions, only kindness.

Later, during my engineering days, Saidhulu and Baskar played a similar role. Whenever I needed help navigating the large and unfamiliar campus, they ensured I reached wherever I needed to go. Their support was not loud or visible, but it was deep.

Academically too, I was never left to figure things out alone. Professor Prasad, who was then the Head of the CSE department, went out of his way to include me in the classroom experience. During Theory of Computation classes, he would draw tactile representations of abstract concepts and explain them aloud, ensuring I learned alongside everyone else, not separately. That effort told me I belonged there as much as anyone.

Many other faculty members supported me in ways that rarely made it into records or reports. Indhira Madam, Adhilakshmi Madam, Rajeshwari Madam, and Professor Karunakumar ensured that explanations never stopped where accessibility began. Ravindhrababu Sir, who was the Dean of Student Affairs, stood out for his constant encouragement. Even today, whenever I find myself in need of guidance, his support continues to light the way.

Professor Kameshwara Rao, Madhusudhan Sir, Dhanalakshmi Madam, Sandhya Rani Madam, and Swapna Madam contributed in their own ways, adjusting teaching styles, clarifying doubts, and never making me feel like a burden.

Equally important were the scribes assigned to me during exams. Many of them were from non-technical backgrounds, they listened carefully, wrote patiently, and became extensions of my intent. Nazima and Kanakadurga, both from non-CSE streams, stood out for their sincerity and dedication. They helped translate my knowledge onto paper with care and clarity, ensuring that my answers reflected my understanding.

The affection shown by each and everyone remains priceless to me. They asked for nothing and expected nothing. They simply showed up when it mattered.

By the end of that punishing year, I was not just a student anymore. I was an engineer in spirit. The fight for ECET had been about entry and the fight in engineering was about existence. What had begun as a fight merely to enter Polytechnic had slowly turned into something far larger. A relentless effort to exist and endure in spaces where no one quite knew how to place me.

Only later did I realize the significance of it. I was a person blind from birth, with 100% vision loss, and I had completed Polytechnic in Andhra Pradesh state. And I was the first person to do so. Not just in my state, but in India. When I completed engineering as well, it became clear that this too had not been done by someone like me.

I didn't see it as an achievement to announce, only as a fact that reshaped what was considered possible.

Years later, Swarnalatha Madam told me something that stopped me in my tracks. During one of my most difficult phases, when finances were tight and dignity mattered deeply, Pavan used his scholarship fees for my expenses. I would have never known if not told.

Some support announces itself; some remains silent until time reveals it. This was the latter.

When I look back, I don't remember only courtrooms or refusals. I remember the subtle sound of circuits, the smell of paper through government printers, the support of my people, and my mother's voice when she said, "You did it."

Many people encouraged me during the legal struggle and in other circumstances, but Pavan stayed through the long pauses. The waiting rooms, the unanswered questions, and the silence between hearings. When outcomes were uncertain, his belief did not waver.

During my 3rd year of engineering, another chapter entered my life. It reminded me that the help we receive does not always end with us. Sometimes, it travels forward.

That is when I met Mr. Subramanyam.

He had lost his sight while studying intermediate, around the year 2000. Seven years later, in 2007, while traveling on a train, he happened to meet a senior student from my college. In the course of a casual conversation, my name came up. A blind engineering student who had somehow fought his way into the system.

That one sentence stayed with him. And it led him to me.

He came to the college searching for me with a simple, almost hesitant question. “How can I complete my B.Com through distance education?”

Until then, he had never touched a computer. He had never heard a screen reader speak. He had no idea that technology could turn silence into voice and uncertainty into confidence.

I introduced him to computers. To JAWS. To the idea that blindness did not have to mean dependence. He learned with determination. Step by step. Key by key.

He completed his education. He attempted competitive examinations. He cleared them.

Today, Mr. Subramanyam works as a Manager at the State Bank of India.

His life did not change because of something extraordinary I gave him. It changed because I chose not to hide what I had learned.

Years later, when my own life entered one of its most difficult phases, it was he who stood beside me. The man who once came to me seeking direction became the one who offered me strength.

That was when I truly understood something important. Support does not end when you receive it. When shared, it becomes a circle. And sometimes, it comes back to hold you when you least expect it.

Those moments were pure, unwavering light. Proof that vision doesn't depend on eyes, it depends on belief.

Chapter 9: From rejections to recognition

By the end of the 3rd year at Gudlavalleru Engineering College, the campus pulsed with an excitement that was almost electric. Placements had begun, a season where students run around with nervousness. Students were to be found under trees and inside the sophisticated college library, reciting formulas, practicing mock interview questions, and reassuring each other.

It was a steep, uncertain mountain for me. I knew I had to climb and cross multiple invisible hurdles to reach my destination.

During placements, Professor Karunakumar, the placement officer, stood firmly by my side. He ensured I was prepared, represented daily, and never sidelined.

While I already fought so many battles just to get into the campus, it was time to fight to step into the world outside.

One day, Wipro Technologies arrived at the campus and transformed the whole vibe. Not only the students but also the faculty presented their best selves.

The first round was an aptitude test.

My scribe sat beside me, her voice clear as she read each question. Logical puzzles, English passages, and number patterns. Questions that most students saw, while I had to hear, interpret, and answer in rhythm with her voice.

When the shortlisted names were announced, my heart thudded as the HR from Wipro read aloud. "Nagababu."

A few students clapped, some seemed surprised. I smiled because even a small victory mattered.

Then was the time of the technical interview. The room smelled faintly of air conditioning and new furniture. Questions came fast. Pointers in C, data structures, and flowcharts. The interviewers were curious, almost intrigued.

One asked, "How do you debug without seeing the screen?"

I replied, "The compiler talks to me. Every error has a sound. I follow the sound. I have to sequentially navigate through code, line by line, using keyboard arrow keys since I don't get a complete view at one time."

He was impressed and said, "Brilliant answer."

The HR round went smoothly too. It was about challenges, teamwork, and communication. I walked out feeling light and hopeful.

That evening, results were announced. A roar of cheers filled the hall, and dozens of names were announced. There was joy and chaos. I waited but my name did not come up.

A quiet ache settled in my chest. Later, the placement officer approached. "Wipro has not rejected you, Nagababu. Your result is on hold. That's all we know."

It wasn't rejection; it was silence. And sometimes, silence is just destiny catching its breath.

Days passed, every morning I asked, "Any update?" And every evening, the placement officer said, "Nothing yet."

Then one humid afternoon, he burst into our classroom, breathless but smiling. "Nagababu! Wipro wants to take your telephonic interview. Tonight!"

My pulse rushed. That evening, just as the campus slipped into a soft orange dusk, the landline rang. "Hello, this is Wipro's technical team. Are you ready, Nagababu?"

"Yes, sir."

Then questions were shot like arrows. Logical, algorithms, real-time problem-solving questions. I answered each with clarity.

"How would you work with interfaces that aren't visually accessible?"

"By understanding logic, imagining layout, architecture, and design."

He chuckled, "Good answer."

Two more calls came that week. One for technical validation, another for HR. Then, they didn't say much. No confirmations, no promises. But something in their tone changed. I felt the conversation was warmer and more settled.

I didn't know the result yet. But I allowed myself to feel that I might have crossed the line.

A few days later, the offer letter was rolled out to me. I called my mother and listened to her joyful voice. "See, I told you... Your hard work is stronger than any wall."

For the first time in years, I felt content for allowing myself to dream without fear.

A few months later, I attended L&T's off-campus drive at KL University. Humid hallways, long queues, and anxious faces everywhere.

I cleared the written test and the technical round. In the HR round, the conversation was warm until one interviewer paused and said gently, "You have done exceptionally well. But practically, it might not be feasible."

That word "feasible" carried a sting wrapped in politeness.

"We will get back to you," he concluded.

They never did. Some doors don't close loudly. They just disappear.

Next came the Emphasis drive at Godavari Institute of Engineering and Technology, Rajahmundry.

Nearly 1,500 students appeared for the written test. Around 100 cleared it. After multiple interview rounds, 23 candidates were selected. I was the only blind candidate among them.

I received a letter of intent. Hope filled me like morning sunlight.

Then came the 2008 global recession. Hiring froze. Emails stopped. Promises vanished.

My mother asked gently each night, “Any update?”

I smiled, hiding the ache. “Maybe tomorrow, Amma.”

But tomorrow didn’t come.

Amidst all these struggles, there was another responsibility steering my life. My younger sister, Shailaja.

Unlike me and my other sister, she was not blind. She was bright but struggled with mathematics and drifted toward commerce. After her 12th, we faced a question that felt heavier than any exam.

How do we secure her future when we could barely secure our present?

My father’s support was almost nonexistent. A gap that had been there all our lives. So, like every burden at home, this too came to me.

It was June 2008. I was earning very little, running the computer center, teaching as a lecturer, supporting my mother, and still trying to find my own direction. Yet when it came to Shailaja, I didn’t hesitate.

There was a night I sat alone and thought, “If needed, I will stop my studies. Let her go ahead.”

Not as a sacrifice, but as my responsibility.

Fortunately, with the help of my friend Kalishekar, who was then studying at Madras Christian College, we managed to get her admitted there. Somehow, she completed her graduation. She later found a job and began earning for herself.

While my wait was turning unbearable, I chose to make a move. Principal Srinivas Rao of Sri Srinivasa Degree College in Vuyyuru offered me a lecturer position without any hesitation or doubt.

“Teach them well, Nagababu,” he said. “You will do wonders.”

I thought about it and gave it a try. In my first class, I was not nervous at all. My voice became my vision.

After the class, a student approached me, “Sir, you make us see code like a story.” That sentence was my first true paycheck.

As a side hustle, I also opened a small computer training center beside our house where I spent evenings. Just two rooms. A few second-hand systems. A dozen eager minds. It was the financial support of Anil Sir and Pavan whose timely help made it possible for me to turn a fragile idea into a working space for learning and hope.

The soft thrum of CPUs, the clack of keyboards, and the faint smell of heated circuits. Those became the heartbeat of my evenings. Power cuts were frequent. But I would laugh and say, “Let’s learn logic in the dark. I’ve been doing it for years.”

Laughter filled the room, warming the dim glow of emergency lamps. That center wasn't just about computers. It was about courage, ours and mine.

During the summers of 2008 and 2009, my work went beyond the small center. I began freelancing with Sai Medha Institute, coaching Polytechnic final-year students for the ECET examination. I trained them in core subjects, problem-solving, and exam strategy, the same way I learned to break complexity into logic.

When results came, I was glad to know that several of my students secured good ranks and earned engineering admissions. Watching them move forward reminded me of something important. That even when my own future felt uncertain, I was capable of shaping someone else's.

During those turbulent months, one voice became my world. Rekha. She was my student in the computer training center and also a student of Sri Srinivasa Degree College in Vuyyuru.

She brought notes, assignments, and quiet cheer. "Sir, don't you ever feel tired?" she once asked.

"Tired? Of course. But if I stop walking, who will show others that a path exists?"

Her soft chuckle felt like a lantern in a storm. Without realizing it, she became a calm presence in my hard times. A reminder that sometimes strength arrives disguised as warmth. She didn't change my world, she secured it.

During those months, one incident shook me from deep inside. One evening, in the middle of class, someone shouted outside, "Nagababu! Your mother's been taken to the hospital!"

I ran barefoot through the streets to Pinnamaneni Nursing Home. The same place where my life began. She had consumed acid, worn down by hardships she had carried too long.

The doctor said gravely, “We’ll try our best.”

I handed him 1,500 rupees, my entire earnings from the center. He pressed it back into my hand. “Keep it. She needs you strong.”

I stayed beside her for days. Machines beeped. The air smelled of antiseptic. Every moment felt like a held breath.

When she finally opened her eyes and whispered, “Nani…” I broke down completely. It was forgiveness, love, and rebirth. It was a second chance for both of us.

The responsibility of the family stayed on my shoulders, fully and constantly. My mother. My sisters. Their education. Their safety. Their lives. I carried them all while building a life that didn’t yet feel stable under my own feet.

I never wanted sympathy for any of it. Life doesn't pause for our struggles. You move, even when the weight threatens to bend you. Those years shaped me. Not through comfort, but through load. Not through support, but through absence of it.

It was June 2009. A hot morning. A routine check of my inbox.

And then, the subject line that froze my breath: "Wipro Technologies: Joining Date Confirmation."

"Amma!" I shouted. She ran in panic, and I laughed through tears.

"I'm joining Wipro! It's here finally!" She hugged me tight, whispering, "Delay is not denial, Nani."

That day, even the world felt lighter. My farewell was not in a grand hall. It was inside my small computer center. The same room that had become a refuge for many dreams, including mine. Students from the degree college and the center crowded in. A student read what was written on the blackboard, "Congratulations, Sir. Wipro Awaits You!"

Students filled the room with applause, snacks, stories, and warmth. One student said, "Sir, we wanted to celebrate you where it all began."

When it was my turn to speak, I said quietly, "Strength isn't about sight. It's about vision. You don't need eyes to see your path. Only faith to walk through it."

The room went still and then erupted in applause.

Later that night, I turned off each computer one by one. The screens went dark, but inside me, a light burned brighter than ever.

Chapter 10: When courage found its workplace

The last week of December 2009 settled softly over Hyderabad. I could feel the cold in the air before I even stepped outside. The mornings carried a serene stillness with birds stitching their songs and waking the city. Even without seeing it, I knew the season had changed.

I stood before the towering gates of Wipro Technologies, fingertips brushing the raised letters on my fresh ID card. The cool plastic felt unreal, as if I were touching a dream.

Beyond the security gate, a new world unfolded. The whirring of computers, hurried conversations, and the footsteps blended into a steady rhythm. That sound was layered, steady, and alive. It was the sound of arrival. This wasn't merely a job. It was the door I had knocked on for years, and at last, it had opened.

Inside the induction hall, everything smelled new. Fresh paint, warm manuals, and the aroma of strong coffee. Rows of computers blinked awake as my screen reader's metallic voice greeted me, "Welcome to Wipro Learning Portal."

In a space built entirely for sight, that familiar synthetic tone became my compass. I memorized shortcuts, traced every menu in my mind, and built mental maps of interfaces I couldn't see. When others looked at diagrams projected on screens, I listened for patterns in the trainer's speech. When their eyes scanned the code, I interpreted the same in sound and logic.

A trainee once leaned over and chuckled, "Do you really understand all that at this speed?"

I smiled. "That's the sound of my eyes."

For two and a half months, life became a cycle of early mornings filled with syntax and late nights filled with small triumphs. Each new concept felt like a doorway, and every success whispered the same message, "You are moving forward."

After the training period, I was assigned to my first live project: Nokia's Mobile Broadcast Solution.

And that's when I met Prabhakar, my manager. He was a man of calm speech and purposeful silence. When I first entered his cabin, he said, "Nagababu, I've read about your journey. You have come far. Let's see how far we can go together."

No hesitation. No pity. Just mutual respect.

Within a week, he coordinated with IT to install JAWS on my system. He made sure I was added to every team thread, every meeting, and every update.

When someone suggested assigning me lighter documentation tasks, he responded firmly. “He is a developer. He will write codes, not notes.”

That single sentence shifted how the team saw me, and more importantly, how I saw myself. He assigned me backend modules, integration logic, and real deliverables.

When I completed a deliverable, he didn’t shower praise. He just nodded and said, “Good. Now build the next one.”

A few months into the project, something significant happened. One complete and critical module of the application was handed over to me. It was not a small enhancement or a side task but a core component that the system depended on.

I built it step by step, listening to every dependency, tracing every flow through sound and logic. When the module was integrated and demonstrated, it worked cleanly. End-to-end. That moment was not about proving that a blind developer could work. It was about proving that trust, when placed rightly, multiplies capabilities.

Sometimes, late in the evening, when only the air conditioners buzzed, he would pause by my desk. “Long day, Nagababu?”

“Just fixing a few logical errors, sir.”

He would laugh softly. “That’s all software ever is, fixing logic until it listens to you.”

From him, I learned that true leadership isn’t loud. It’s simple trust that lifts people higher.

If Prabhakar was the wind behind me, Ravikiran, my immediate lead, was my navigator who guided my steps. He had a rare gift of patience that didn’t just wait but understood.

When whiteboards filled with complex flow diagrams I couldn't see, he stayed back after hours. "Okay, Nagababu," he would say gently. "This module sends packets here… that one handles encoding… this connects to the broadcast node…"

He drew shapes in the air I couldn't see, but I heard his explanations and built the picture in my mind.

The sound of distant typing, the murmur of fading conversations, and the drone of machines. All of it blended with his generous explanations. Through him, I discovered something profound. Collaboration doesn't need sight. It needs clarity, patience, and trust.

When the first payday came, the office buzzed with excitement. Everyone refreshed their accounts, smiling at their very first salaries.

Except me.

Days passed. Then weeks. My salary didn't arrive.

The reason? "HDFC requires additional verification for visually challenged employees."

I smiled politely since I was now used to these hiccups. I had to undergo additional steps and wait.

After 40 days, a message arrived on my phone. Salary credited. It felt like a victory. It was proof that I had made it to the world I once thought was closed to people like me. For a moment, those delays, extra procedures, and explanations felt worth it.

But life doesn't pause long on victories. Within a few weeks, I had to take care of a few responsibilities at home, so I applied for a personal loan. There was no response, not even an acknowledgement. So I wrote a firm yet respectful email. It was not to customer support but directly to the managing director of HDFC Bank.

I quoted RBI guidelines, described the discrimination, explained my situation, and ended with, "This isn't about an account. It is about equal respect."

A week later, I received a call. "Mr. Nagababu, your loan is sanctioned. We apologize for the delay."

Sometimes dignity doesn't arrive freely. You must fight for it. Not loudly, but firmly.

Just as the bank had shown resistance, my workplace showed the opposite. A support that was natural, not forced. And at the center of that was Prabhakar.

He believed inclusion did not end at code reviews. "Nagababu, you are joining us today. No excuses," he insisted during team outings. Golf. Adventure games. Things I had only heard of, never imagined participating in.

He once placed a golf club in my hand. "Feel the weight," he said. "Now swing."

The soft thud of the ball flying into the distance, followed by cheers, was more than sight could ever offer.

At pools, restaurants, and parks, they never treated me differently. No awkwardness, no pity. Just presence and true inclusion. I laughed louder than I had in years, visited places I never imagined I would step in, and let conversation, food, and shared moments carry me without hesitation.

At Wipro, months turned into a year. My codes became sharper. I began mentoring interns. Colleagues never introduced me as 'the visually impaired developer.'

They always said, "This is Nagababu, he is brilliant with logic." That shift, from limitation to identity, was one of my most meaningful victories.

When I look back at my first year at Wipro, it doesn't feel like the beginning of a career. It feels like the beginning of belief. Through all the noise of corporate life, the pressure, the delayed salaries, and the uncertainty, one voice remained constant.

Rekha.

My former student who had slowly become the calm in my storms. Though her family didn't approve, she stood with me in the ways she could. No drama. No rebellion. Just quiet conviction, like a lamp that doesn't flicker even when the wind howls.

Every evening, she would ask on call, "Did you eat? Or are you debugging hunger again?" If I was overwhelmed, she sensed it before I said a word. Sometimes we talked for hours about everything and nothing.

Other times, she simply listened. Her silence was heavy with understanding. Her belief steadied me. She didn't fight my battles. She made me strong enough to fight them myself.

Sometimes strength doesn't shout. It arrives in whispers.

Every keystroke, every challenge, and every triumph at Wipro carried the imprint of the people who refused to limit me. Prabhakar's unwavering trust, Ravikiran's patient guidance, and Rekha's quiet strength.

Success is not about who opens a door for you. It is about how you walk through it, with courage, gratitude, and purpose.

Wipro was more than a workplace. It was the first place that did not just see me, it listened to me. And that's how my true beginning began.

There comes a time when life stops testing you with storms and starts teaching you through stillness. Rekha entered my life that way. Not as a turning point, but as a presence that didn't shake, even when everything else did.

Chapter 11: A life built in soft strength

It was around September 2009 when Rekha went to her cousin's place that was in another town. For the first time in a long while, she was not around the institute.

No familiar footsteps, no gentle voice asking if I had eaten. No casual conversations that had become the life of my routine.

Days passed. One, two, three, and four. There were no messages, no calls. Just silence.

At first, I told myself that it was normal. People travel, life pauses, and resumes. But something in me refused to settle.

I noticed her absence everywhere. In the computer center, during evenings, the time started to stretch longer than usual.

I would finish my work and instinctively think of sharing something with her, only to remember she was not there. I replayed her soft giggles in my mind, her warm presence, and the way she listened to me without interrupting. And that was when it became clear. I was not just missing a person, I was missing her.

Those days changed something within me. They stripped away confusion and left behind clarity. Somewhere between the waiting and silence, I acknowledged what my heart had been trying to tell me.

This was not attachment. This was not comfort. This was love, undeniable.

On the night of 26th September 2009, during a phone call, I finally said what had been resting silently in my heart for days, "If we feel the same," I said, "maybe we should stay together. Not as a story, but as a life."

There was no drama. No noise. Just a pause. And then her breath softened.

After she returned, she came to meet me. We spoke, not excitedly, not nervously, but honestly.

She said, “Okay.” That single word felt heavier than any poem.

In December 2009, when I joined Wipro, life finally began to feel stable. By mid-March 2010, my training was completed. Around that time, I went to Chilkur temple alone. Not to ask for success, not to ask for comfort. I prayed only for one thing. That we should live a life together.

The next morning, she called. “My family is looking for a match,” she said quietly.

Our original plan was to wait. To let her complete her master's. To give life more time. But reality stood firmly in front of us. I was blind. I was still early in my career. We both knew what her family would think.

For a while, we believed we could convince them. Then we understood something more difficult. We didn’t need permission to be honest with our hearts. So we chose clarity over fear.

We chose each other. Rekha left her family behind. In fact, she left everything of hers to spend the rest of her life with me.

It was 2nd April 2010, a simple, tranquil evening in Hyderabad. Nothing grand, nothing unusual. Just an ordinary day that felt special only to us.

We arrived at a small neighborhood temple. Just me, Rekha, my grandmother, and close friends have come by car from Vuyyuru.

The air was filled with the scent of sandalwood, camphor, and jasmine.

There were no crowds or decorations. Only a few familiar voices, quiet prayers, and the steady presence of those who stood with us as our life together began.

My grandmother's presence alone felt like a blessing. My family had agreed in their hearts, but not with their presence.

The priest's chants rose and fell like waves, the sound of conch shells echoing in the background. Then I heard Rekha approaching. The soft rustle of silk, the faint jingle of bangles. Her breath was steady yet slightly nervous.

There were no cameras or decorations. Just two hearts, ready to make a promise.

When I held the mangalasutram, a yellow thread of commitment in Indian culture, it felt sacred. It was like holding the weight of responsibility and love together. I tied it around her neck with quiet reverence.

For a brief moment, everything stopped, the chanting, the temple bells, even my heartbeat. That silence wasn't empty; it was full. The sound of two lives aligning.

My grandmother placed her soft, wrinkled palms on our heads. Her blessing carried the strength. She didn't say much, but her touch told us everything, "You are not alone anymore." That was enough.

A few days later, we boarded a train to Chennai. Not to celebrate luxury as newlyweds, but to find peace after years of struggle. To sit beside each other without explanations, without timelines pressing our backs.

The compartment smelled of steel and fresh coffee. Vendors called out, "Masala vadai, kaapi, kaapi!" Masala vadai refers to lentil fritters, while kaapi is South Indian filter coffee.

The rhythm of the trains' wheels felt soothing. Metal against the track felt like a heartbeat of motion. Repeating. Reliable. Almost reassuring. It sounded like a heart that knew where it was going, even if it didn't know the destination.

We spoke about small things at first. What we would eat next. How long the journey would take. Who might be waiting at the other end. Then slowly, without realizing it, the conversations deepened.

Rekha described what passed outside the window. Banana trees swaying in the wind, fishermen repairing their nets, and children waving as the train roared past.

Each description felt like a gift. Not just of sight, but trust. She was letting me see the world through her words, and I was learning not just with my ears but with presence.

The next morning, we visited Marina Beach, and the world widened. The sea breeze carried laughter, freedom, and stories in every wave. The air smelled of salt and freedom.

We walked slowly, the cool sand shifting beneath our feet, the waves brushing against us.
Rekha smiled and said, "The sea doesn't ask who you are. It just comes and goes."

We didn’t need to talk much. The silence was enough. The breeze carried all the words we couldn’t say.

That journey wasn’t a honeymoon. It was a pause between storms, a moment where time finally stopped chasing us.

Back in Hyderabad, on 13th April 2010, we went to the Arya Samaj to formally register our marriage. The priest recited Sanskrit verses, each syllable crisp and measured. Papers rustled softly. Ink dried patiently.

One of my close friends had come with us to stand as a witness. He was blind too. There was a brief pause at the table. The staff looked at the papers, then at him, and gently said that they cannot accept his signature as a witness.

There was no argument. No scene. Only a quiet postponement. We returned the next day with another friend to complete the process.

When I signed the register, I felt the raised government seal under my fingers. Rough, cold, and unmistakably real. In that quiet moment, love became legality. Faith gained form.

There was no crowd. No ceremony. Just legitimacy, documented.

We stepped out holding hands, aware that nothing about our lives would become easier overnight. But confident that whatever followed would be faced together.

We moved into a modest two-room flat near my office. It was not large, but it was ours. The space shaped not by furniture, but by hope.

Every corner had something to speak of. The kitchen whispered in the whistle of the pressure cooker. The steel tumblers chimed like small bells in a household temple. Rekha's bangles created a soft rhythm like the music of a home learning its heartbeat. And my laptop keys clicked into the night like tiny footsteps chasing our future.

Mornings began with the smell of coffee and curry leaves. Evenings ended with laughter and the soft sound of my laptop as she read recipes and stories aloud beside me.

A small dining table by the window became our cozy corner. Two plates, two cups, and one honest conversation at a time.

Some evenings, she returned from work and handed me a cold Fanta from the shop downstairs.

"Cheers, Nani," she would say lightly.

“Yes,” I’d smile.” “And how’s the sunset today?”

“Orange melting into purple, like your code when it finally runs without errors,” she would laugh.

We had little but lacked nothing essential. They were ordinary days that felt extraordinary.

The years that followed tested us. Salaries were meager to take care of a family of five. Bills waited patiently. Futures remained uncertain.

But Rekha never stepped back. She took responsibility without resentment. She balanced work, home, and uncertainty with clarity.

When I worked late or returned home drained, she didn’t ask for explanations. She waited with companionship, not pressure.

On nights when the city outside slept, we sat together in the dim light of our living room. Her head resting on my shoulder, her quiet presence saying everything words could not.

“We are okay. We will get through this.”

Her laughter became my dawn. Her patience, my horizon.

Looking back now, I understand our marriage was never about defiance. It was never rebellion against tradition or family.

It was a quiet affirmation that love does not seek permission. It asks only for honesty and courage. We didn't challenge the world loudly. We lived truthfully.

Rekha became more than my partner. She became my balance, my still point, the rhythm beneath my racing life. Our home held no luxury, but it carried meaning. Woven from shared effort, steady faith, and countless small gestures.

Our first wedding anniversary arrived on 2nd April 2011, carrying with it a coincidence that felt almost poetic. That evening, India played the World Cup final. The house filled with voices, laughter, and the rising volume of the television commentary.

Friends and a few close relatives gathered around, reacting to every run and wicket. Cheers burst out without warning, then silence followed, and somewhere between the commentator's excitement and the crowd's roar, our personal celebration merged effortlessly with the national one.

I didn’t feel like two events were happening side by side. It felt like one shared joy, unfolding through sound, emotion, and togetherness.

When the final moments came, the commentary cracked with emotion, and then the room erupted. People clapped, shouted, and hugged one another. I didn’t need to see the trophy lifted to know what had happened. I could hear it in the voices.

For me, the moment carried something deeper. My favorite cricketer, Sachin Tendulkar, had finally reached the moment the nation had waited for. Listening to the way his name was spoken that night, with reverence and relief, felt like hearing gratitude itself.

Sitting beside Rekha, surrounded by shared happiness, I felt an overwhelming sense of completeness. My love for cricket, my admiration for Sachin, my friendships, and my marriage all came together that evening. Some anniversaries are marked by dates. Ours was marked by sound, emotion, and the joy of being where we were meant to be.

This phase taught me that love is not something you see. It is something you feel. In patience, in presence, in belief that does not ask for proof.

Chapter 12: Beyond stability, towards meaning

The years after marriage did not rush forward; they moved like calm waves.

By 2013, the corridors of Wipro had become my second home. I no longer needed to be introduced to the sounds that filled my days. The soft beep of access cards, the low vibrations of servers, and the occasional burst of laughter from a nearby cubicle formed the soundtrack of my everyday life.

Deadlines no longer tightened my breath. Reviews no longer unsettled me. Client calls felt less like tests and more like conversations. I had earned my place by being consistent.

And yet, amidst the comfort, a quiet thought began to surface. Not restlessness. Not dissatisfaction. But a calm question returned to me more often than I expected.

'You have proven that you can survive here, Nagababu. Now what do you want to build?"

It was not ambition speaking, it was readiness.

In November 2012, I interviewed for Infosys. I didn't see it as an escape, but a progression. A chance to test whether what I had learned could hold up beyond familiarity.

The offer letter arrived in the last week of November. Rekha read it aloud to me, slowly, as she always did with important things.

"Posting: Mahindra World City, Chennai." She then paused.

"That's far, Nani."

I smiled, already sensing the weight behind distance.

"Yes," I said gently. "Sometimes distance teaches us what proximity never can."

She didn't argue. She never did when she felt something was right for us. Her silence was not hesitation, it was trust.

Chennai greeted me with unfamiliar rhythms. Everything demanded adjustment. Work schedules, commute, living arrangements, and long evenings that felt quieter without Rekha by my side.

During those early days in Chennai, help arrived quietly, through family and extended kindness.

My paternal uncle, Durgarao, introduced me to Vasundhara and family, part of his close circle. They welcomed me without questions, the way people do when help feels natural rather than charitable. For the first couple of days, I stayed at their home. Those nights mattered more than I can explain.

In an unfamiliar city, having a place where voices were warm and meals were shared made all the difference. They helped me with food, boarding, and the small logistics that otherwise feel heavy when you are starting from scratch.

Through them, I was introduced to Mr. Hari, who worked at Infosys. That connection became crucial. From the very first day, he made sure I was not alone in the city.

On my first morning, I didn't navigate the Infosys office bus on my own. Mr. Hari took me along with him, guiding me through the routine, the stops, and the rhythm of a workday that was still new to me. That simple act removed a fear I hadn't spoken aloud.

Beyond work, he helped me settle into Chennai itself. Finding a house, understanding neighborhoods, dealing with landlords. Things that become overwhelming when you don't know a city and cannot rely on sight. He stood beside me through those decisions, patient and steady.

Looking back, it was not just assistance, it was reassurance. The kind that tells you that you belong here too.

The Infosys campus at Mahindra World City had its own energy. Not loud, but expansive. The steady beep of turnstiles, footsteps converging into long corridors, and the measured rush of people moving with purpose. It all created a feeling of constant motion.

Professionally, the learning curve was steep. Systems were complex. Tools assumed visual interaction. Dashboards were crowded with information that was inaccessible to me. Once again, I found myself returning to an old skill, adaptation.

I rebuilt workflows in my head. I memorized shortcuts the way others remembered icons. I listened for patterns, wrote down shortcut sequences by sound, and memorized every pathway through rhythm and repetition.

Once a colleague asked, genuinely curious, “How do you manage all this without seeing the screen?”

I answered, “By learning to trust sound, following sequence, and having patience.”

It was not a clever response. It was a lived truth through practice.

Chennai tested my endurance, but I was missing Hyderabad, my home. More than the city, I missed Rekha.

Loneliness is a strange thing. It doesn’t always arrive loudly. Sometimes it slips in quietly between work calls, during late dinners eaten alone, or in the silence of a room that doesn’t carry her voice.

There were evenings when the laptop keys clicked beneath my fingers, and yet something felt incomplete. I would imagine Rekha folding clothes back home, or singing softly while preparing dinner, or simply waiting near the window the way she always did when she sensed I was having a long day.

Distance does something peculiar to love. It stretches it, shapes it, sharpens it.

Our conversations became shorter but heavier with meaning. Her gentle "How was your day?" carried more warmth than a thousand words.

Sometimes she stayed silent on the call, and even that silence felt like companionship. I realized then. You don't miss a person because they are far. You miss them because their presence has become your rhythm.

And with each passing week, the ache of that missing grew a little deeper, a little clearer. Until one evening, as I sat alone in my small Chennai room, listening to the distant sounds of the city, I understood what my heart had been whispering all along.

It was time to go back. That's when I sat before the system, typed my transfer request, and under 'Reason,' wrote two words: Personal grounds.

Weeks later, my inbox chimed. "Transfer to Hyderabad Development Center approved."

I was glad and started to pack my belongings and booked a train for myself.

The train back felt lighter than any I had taken before. At Secunderabad, when I smelled the tea and samosas, the crisp, triangular fried snacks filled with spiced potato, I knew I was back where I belonged.

When I reached home, Rekha's hand found mine. Firm, warm, and reassuring, it felt like home.

Back in Hyderabad, Infosys placed me on a backend automation project. Layered, logical, and demanding focus rather than visibility.

It suited me. I liked the workdays that had structure. My focus was entirely on codes. I chased the bugs with patience and not panic. One fix led calmly to the next.

At different points in my career, both during my first stint at Infosys and later at Wipro, I encountered a quieter challenge. Not rejection, but hesitation. A few managers, unfamiliar with how I worked, chose not to assign me to certain projects. It was not malice. It was uncertainty and, sometimes, a lack of willingness to explore what was possible.

At Infosys, I was once told that a particular client environment, Cisco, might not support screen readers and that approvals could take time. The conversion ended there. A door closed, not because I lacked skill, but because no one wanted to push the question forward.

Years later, at Wipro, I found myself working with Cisco as a client again. This time, not only was the screen reader support available, but it was excellent. The same ecosystem that once felt inaccessible now welcomed me without friction. Ironically, when I returned to Infosys later, I worked with the same client again.

That contrast taught me something important. Sometimes, opportunities are denied not because of limitations, but because of assumptions. Not because systems can't adapt, but because people hesitate to ask.

During my later years at Infosys, I worked closely with Sudhakar, an architect whose thinking matched depth with openness. Our conversations were never short. We spoke about technology, system design, health, society, and often about life itself.

Even today, whenever we connect, the calls stretch long, not out of habit, but out of curiosity. Working with him reminded me that true collaboration doesn't begin with accommodation. It begins with respect.

One day, after a long debugging session, my manager remarked lightly, "You make silence productive."

I smiled. "It's where I've always worked best."

Home and work no longer pulled in different directions. Life settled into a quiet zone. Shared meals, a steady routine, and evenings that allowed room for conversation.

But life rarely stays still for long. In 2014, I attempted the IBPS (Institute of Banking Personnel Selection) PO (Probationary Officer) examination. I gave the test without any high expectation. Months later, the result arrived, and I had cleared it. Not just clearing the exam, but I also received an appointment letter in September 2014 for the PO role at Andhra Bank.

For many, bank jobs are a dream since they are secure and respectable jobs.

But I stood at the crossroads. One path offered stability. The other offered passion.

I had to choose passion since I worked too hard to earn my engineering degree. I went through rejections, setbacks, and limitations. Technology was not just a job for me, but it was a space where I had built myself from scratch.

I discussed it with Rekha, my well-wishers, weighing every possibility. Finally, clarity emerged. I choose tech.

And with that choice, I stepped forward again.

Someone I trusted told me, “Wipro has an opening that suits your skillset. You should apply.”

Though the suggestion came casually, it carried possibility. I applied, and a few weeks later, the confirmation arrived. I was selected.

Joining back Wipro in March 2015 felt like coming home, but this time, I carried more than experience. I carried a clearer purpose and deeper resilience. I was coming back as someone who has rebuilt himself through adaptation and persistence.

Within a few months of rejoining, I was moved to the CISCO project. It was a significant shift. It demanded patience, precision, and the ability to think in structure rather than visuals.

The Cisco project spanned continents. It dealt with partner systems, royalty models, and automation workflows that were complex, interwoven, and demanding precision. Deadlines were sharp, and expectations were high.

But I had changed. Pressure no longer frightened me. It made me focused.

Once, during a long troubleshooting session, a teammate joked, “Sir, when you say ‘Let’s check the logs,’ even the errors seem to calm down.”

I laughed. “Logs are like people. They speak, if you listen long enough.”

While I was enjoying my work at Wipro, another incident jolted us. And naturally, another hope took shape.

By 2015, Rekha and I began to imagine the next chapter of our lives. Not loudly, not hurriedly. Just gently. We wanted our family to grow.

Weeks turned into months. Anticipation slowly gave way to questions. We kept visiting hospitals on weekends. But reports always arrived with words that balanced possibility and uncertainty.

Rekha dealt with every situation calmly. “Maybe next time,” she would say every time. Her voice carried strength, though I could sense her pain.

In May 2016, silence returned, heavier than before. A miscarriage.

The word itself felt inadequate for what it took from us. That night, the house seemed to hold its breath. Rekha held my hand and whispered, “It’s okay, Nani. Maybe this wasn’t the time.”

Her strength did two things. Broke me and held me at the same time.

We did not let go of hope. We placed it deeper, beneath patience, beneath acceptance, beneath faith that no longer demanded answers.

Four months later, in October 2016, when silence had felt permanent, the pregnancy test carried a different weight in our hands. We waited without excitement, almost defensively, as though hope itself needed permission to return.

Then it happened. The test was positive.

Rekha's voice trembled as she told me, a smile and a tear sharing the same breath. Neither of us reacted immediately. We didn't celebrate. We whispered gratitude instead.

From that day on, time began to move differently. Slower. More deliberate. Every visit to the doctor felt like a ritual. Each scan was like a sacred pause. When we heard the faint and real heartbeat, it felt less like sound and more like confirmation that life was willing to try again.

Knowing how fragile Rekha's condition was, I requested Wipro for work-from-home from Vuyyuru. I expected resistance since it was not common in those days. But they agreed. That decision felt like grace.

That decision meant more to me than any award or promotion. It was corporate compassion but deeply human at heart.

As the months passed, fear slowly loosened its grip. Caution remained, but hope had learned to stay.

Around this time, life reminded me once again that blindness doesn't limit what I can do. It only changes how I do it. During Rekha's 6th and 7th months of pregnancy, our days in Vuyyuru were quiet but demanding. Most of the time, it was just three of us. Rekha, my grandmother, and me. We were learning to move through this fragile phase with both fear and faith sitting beside us.

Naveen and a few close friends helped us in every possible way. They sometimes got meals, arranged medicines, and made sure we had everything we required. I remember how Naveen, even though he was not financially strong, supported me a lot.

And Pavan had sent rice bags a couple of times. Those acts were of love, translated through touch, patience, and presence.

Careers brought distance and responsibilities, but time never diluted Pavan's support. It just matured. Less visible, more dependable.

By June 2017, Rekha's due date drew near. With every passing day, excitement and anxiety travelled together, refusing to walk alone. The monsoon arrived early that year. We could hear rain gather on rooftops, pooling in familiar places, mixed with our expectations.

Her doctor, Dr. Karuna at Time Hospital, had been with us throughout this journey. Over time, trust had replaced fear.

"We'll try for a normal delivery," she said calmly. "Let's give it a chance."

On the night of June 7, around 9:30 p.m., Rekha's contractions began.

Hospital corridors carried their own language. Rushed footsteps, hushed instructions, the steady sound of medical equipment, and the sharp scent of disinfectant that announces seriousness. Hours passed. Rekha labored with quiet strength, guided by Dr. Karuna's firm and reassuring voice.

Outside, I paced the corridor, counting steps without realizing it. Each round ended in the same silent prayer, "Please keep them both safe."

My friend Himashankar was there with me throughout. Along with my grandmother and Naveen at the hospital. Their presence helped me manage my anxiety that had been building inside me. We stood together in the dim corridor, bound by worry, hope, and anticipation of a new life.

My grandmother also tried to tell the doctor to go with a C-section to let Rekha out of trouble and pain.

Near midnight, Dr. Karuna stepped out. “The baby is fine,” she said gently, “but it isn’t progressing. We’ll need to do a C-section.”

And then, on June 8th, 2017, the night opened with a sound that changed everything. A newborn’s cry, soft at first, then full and certain.

A nurse came out smiling, saying, “It’s a girl!”

June 8. My birthday. Her birthday.

Two lives folded neatly into one dawn.

Inside, Dr. Karuna said warmly, “Both are safe, Nagababu. She’s strong, and so is Rekha.”

Rekha’s tired voice found me. “She came on your birthday.”

I held her hand. "Then she's twice my life."

The nurse placed our daughter beside Rekha and prepared the first bottle feed. She explained to me how to do it. From then on, it was always me who mixed the formula carefully, checked the temperature, and fed my daughter.

The simple act of holding her, steadying the bottle, and feeling her tiny breaths became the first moment I truly understood. Blindness does not limit fatherhood, I can do everything.

We named her Nithyanandhika, meaning eternal joy.

When I held my daughter for the first time, her warmth against my chest felt unreal and undeniable all at once. Years of waiting, loss, restraint, and fear collapsed into a single truth.

She was here. I couldn't see her. I didn't need to see her. Her breathing, her tiny movements, and her quiet existence told me everything.

Those first days in the hospital were demanding. With no one around during some hours, I learned every small task by doing it myself. I held Rekha's hand as she shifted in bed, helped her sit up slowly after the C-section, and even supported her as she took her first careful bath after surgery.

People assume sight defines caregiving. But care comes from presence, not vision. And in those hours, I proved to myself, and to life, that I could carry my family in every way that mattered.

Outside, morning announced itself in the subtle ways it always does. Quieter streets, softened sounds, a feeling of beginning. It was still June 8. The world had given me life twice.

Joy did not arrive alone.

As days passed and hospital bills accumulated, numbers began to press in from the edges of our happiness. Medical expenses, months of limited income, and ongoing responsibilities formed a quiet, familiar weight.

We didn't panic. We adjusted.

Years of uncertainty had taught us discipline. We cut back where we could, laughed wherever possible, and stretched every rupee further than it seemed capable of going.

Some nights, I lay awake calculating, silently wondering how we would make it through.

Rekha sensed it every time. "We've faced bigger storms, Nani. This is only another tide."

Her calm steadiness kept us afloat. Our love is the only currency that never devalued.

By 2018, my role in Wipro had quietly evolved. I was no longer writing codes. I was guiding others.

From developer to reviewer, from contributor to mentor, from solving problems to helping people believe they could solve them too. I wore many hats.

When a junior engineer panicked, I'd say, "Don't rush. Break it down. Read one line at a time." Their relief told me they heard more than technical advice. Not just about programming, but about life.

Prabhakar's words from my early Wipro days often echoed in my mind, "Reliability isn't in code, Nagababu. It's in consistency."

Leadership, I realized, isn't about authority. It's about creating courage.

And at home, life found its quiet balance.

Rekha's calm voice anchored every storm. Nithyanandhika's laughter brought sunshine to our homes.

Evenings became sacred. After dinner, we would sit near the window while our daughter slept, her breath soft and rhythmic. Outside, the city's gentle noises were like a lullaby meant for adults trying to sleep.

Rekha would describe the sky to me. "Orange melting into violet tonight," she would say. And I would imagine the world. Color by color, sound by sound, like the way I've always known it.

From the heartbreak of 2016 to the miracle of 2017, life taught us one profound truth. Faith doesn't erase struggle. It redeems it. Patiently, quietly, and completely.

Chapter 13: Where home and the world converged

By the time 2019 arrived, life in Vuyyuru had settled into a calm, deliberate beat. After years of motion, resistance, and relentless striving, there was finally a sense of steadiness. Not stagnation, but balance.

One small house stood quietly amid the familiar sounds of the town. Sugarcane leaves rustling in the breeze, distant temple bells marking the hours, bicycles passing by on uneven roads. It had been nearly 3 years since Rekha and I moved here during her pregnancy in 2016. A decision made under pressure, sustained by patience, and shaped by love.

At first, living away from the city felt like a pause. But slowly, I understood it wasn't a pause at all. It was preparation.

Every morning began like a poem written in sound and routine. The sweet smell of milk boiling, the metallic voice of JAWS greeting me from my laptop, and the quick, joyful footsteps of little Nithyanandhika running through the veranda. Not to forget her laughing cutting in between.

Outside, roosters announced the day. Inside, global systems waited for connection. Two worlds coexisted for me. The grounded simplicity of Vuyyuru and the pulse of international technology.

At times, I paused at my desk, letting that realization sink in. Not from a glass tower, but from a quiet room. Guided by sound, rhythm, and an unshakeable will to belong.

My workspace was modest but deeply familiar. A wooden desk that became smooth with years of use. A dependable Wi-Fi router. And a laptop whose keys memorized my fingertips.

After rain, the earthy smell drifted in through the open window, grounding me in where I was even when my mind moved elsewhere. Then came the sound I waited for every morning. “Welcome to Windows. JAWS ready.”

To others it might have sounded mechanical. To me, it was reassurance. A signal that the day had begun and that I was, once again, connected to possibility.

Rekha would quietly place a cup of tea beside the keyboard. “Good luck, Nani,” she would say before turning to help Nithya log into her online class.

In those simple moments, the transformation always struck me. A few keystrokes expanded my small room. My workday spanned different time zones, data centers, and teams I had never physically met. Yet worked alongside every day.

Between the sounds of home and the tune of codes, I realized my life itself had become a bridge. Linking places, people, and possibilities that rarely intersected.

Working from Vuyyuru didn't slow me down. If anything, it sharpened me.

Power cuts arrived without warning and left just as suddenly. But adaptation had long been my practice. A charged hotspot, disciplined routines, and trust in the process became my alternate routine.

Rekha would sometimes stand near the doorway, listening to the steady pattern of my typing. "You work like silence itself," she once said.

She was right. Silence had become my strongest collaborator. Alert, focused, and uninterrupted. While others required movement and noise to think, I found clarity in stillness. Stillness was not emptiness, it was control.

In 2021, COVID entered our home like a silent intruder.

It started with me. Mild fever, fatigue, and a cough that felt heavier than usual. I stepped back and told Rekha not to come near me and to be careful. But caution was no match for proximity. Within a few days, Rekha also tested positive. Then, one by one, everyone in the house was infected.

The peaceful home that had always protected us became a battleground. While my own sickness fluctuated, I was taking care of everyone around me. Managing medications, arranging meals, checking temperatures, and keeping track of oxygen readings. That moment demanded strength, and strength arrived.

My sister Shailaja, along with her husband Manoj, took Nithya and my mother with them and stayed in a different room in the same house. My mother kept cooking tirelessly, sending hot food to keep us going.

With time, though the rest of us were recovering, Rekha's condition began to worsen. Her fever didn't drop. Her breathing grew shallow. I could hear the hesitation in every breath she took.

I called my friend Subhramanyam, and explained the situation. He connected us to Dr. Srilatha, who was a renowned nephrologist guiding many through COVID. She asked us to get Rekha's CT scan done immediately.

Naveen came on his bike, helped Rekha sit behind him, and took her for the scan. He went back and forth, first to get the scan, then to collect the report.

When the CT scan reports arrived, the air in the room shifted. Her SpO2 was at 85. The report showed significant lung infection.

Rekha was reluctant to get admitted. She said, "I don't want to go to the hospital. I'm scared."

I held her hand gently and convinced her, saying, "I know. But we must go. I need you safe more than I need you near."

With that, we left for the hospital.

The second wave was swallowing the country. Beds were rare. Hospitals were overflowing. However, by some grace, TIME Hospital gave her a bed. Just a small shared space. Two beds in a room barely larger than a storeroom. Maybe four feet by eight. I remember sitting against the wall, knees folded, hours turning into days.

Surprisingly, I was not afraid. I don't know where that strength came from. For the first time in my life, I felt stronger than my circumstances.

Doctors and nurses were stretched thin, yet their humanity shone through like light in fog. I could sense their movements, their steady confidence, and their refusal to let fear dictate care.

Dr. Anil, the treating doctor, squeezed my hand and said, "Don't worry, man. You have given me a task, and I am here to do it."

Outside the hospital, support arrived without hesitation. Naveen and my friend Hanuma used to get hot food every day, entering a COVID ward despite not being infected themselves. Inside the room, their voices carried warmth far beyond the walls.

There was one specific injection the doctor insisted was crucial, as Rekha's recovery was slow. The injection was hard to find outside. But somehow, through a chain of contacts and hope, we got it.

Meanwhile, Subhramanyam paid the hospital fees. Insurance was claimed later.

Slowly, the numbers began improving. Her oxygen stabilized. The fever reduced. Her breathing eased.

After two days, Rekha turned toward me and said softly, "Don't sit on the chair. Come sleep beside me."

After six days, she was becoming normal. We survived.

All through these tough days, my sister, Manoj, and grandmother took care of Nithya, who was around three years old.

After returning home, I took over. I remember lifting her gently with a fresh towel wrapped around her, letting her rest her head over my shoulder. She didn't know what had happened, but she sensed we had all fought something big.

Strength doesn't come from eyes. It comes from necessity and love.

In March 2021, while working at Infosys, my life leaned forward again unexpectedly. I had received another offer and, with honesty, informed my manager that I might move on. Instead of resistance, something unexpected happened.

They looked at my work and my consistency and said, “If you are willing to stay, we would match your current offer and nominate you for H-1B.”

It wasn’t a decision I had chased. It was a door that opened because someone saw what I had built in silence. I agreed to stay.

The first lottery results came. My name wasn’t there.

In August 2021, the second round of the lottery arrived. And this time, my nomination was picked. I then submitted the required documentation for processing. Only later did I learn that the case had cleared all internal approvals and was officially ready for the final interview stage.

In October 2021, during a short visit to Hyderabad, life shifted again quietly, unexpectedly. It was 13 October, a heavy, humid night. Rekha and Nithya were asleep beside me, their breathing slow and even, the room filled with the familiar scents of sandalwood and fresh linen.

Around 2 a.m., I woke without knowing why. Half-asleep, I reached for my phone and felt a single notification, Subject: H-1B Nomination: Selected for Processing.

My nomination had been officially approved.

For a few seconds, I didn't move, unsure if I was dreaming. I checked it again, carefully, afraid my hope might outrun reality. Then the meaning landed.

My heart raced. I whispered, almost afraid of the words, "Rekha… it happened. We got selected"

She stirred, smiling even before she was fully awake. "See?" she murmured. "I told you. It would come."

In my excitement, I typed the wrong password repeatedly. Rekha laughed softly. "Slow down, Nani. You will wake Nithya before the sun does."

By 5 a.m. morning, the house was awake. Pinky and Himasankar found me still at the laptop. "Why are you up so early?"

"You won't believe this. The H-1B got selected."

They looked at the screen. That small white email window was glowing brighter than the sunrise.

Rekha leaned over my shoulder; Pinky clapped, and Himasankar laughed. And I just sat there, letting it settle.

That ordinary night had quietly changed the direction of our lives.

Selection, I soon learned, was only the beginning. The months that followed tested every ounce of patience I had. It was the hardest phase. Finding a visa slot.

COVID-19 had slowed the world, and the U.S. Consulate appointments vanished almost instantly.

Every day followed the same pattern. Mornings, I would check the website. Evenings, I would refresh it again, waiting.

Each "No slots available" message felt heavier than the last.

I had learned resilience over years. This phase demanded something else. Endurance without control.

Rekha remained steady throughout. "If it took years to reach here," she said gently, "a few more months won't stop us." She was right.

Finally, after what felt like a lifetime, the long-awaited email arrived: Visa Interview Scheduled, 6th April 2022. The relief felt physical, like breath returning after a long hold.

Even then, a familiar thought lingered in my mind. Experience had trained me to expect resistance. I knew, logically, there would be no hurdles, and yet somewhere inside, I still prepared myself for rejection.

That April morning became a memory etched in gold.

We three, Rekha, Nithya, and I, stood outside the U.S. Consulate in Hyderabad with packed documents in hand. The air carried the mixed smells of wet concrete, paper, and brewing coffee from a nearby stall. Inside, footsteps echoed against marble floors.

Rekha held my hand. Nithya's tiny fingers clutched the other. A volunteer guided us to the counter. The officer's voice was calm and procedural.

"Mr. Jannu, you are with Infosys?"

"Yes, madam. Backend development for Cisco modernization.

"And these are your family members?"

‘Yes, madam.”

There was a soft click of typing. After a few questions and a short pause, she said simply, “All approved. Congratulations.” She added, “Welcome to the United States.”

The impossible finally arrived. Visa approved. It wasn’t just a visa. It was acknowledgement. Proof that quiet perseverance could echo louder than any applause.

For a moment, sound itself seemed suspended. Rekha squeezed my hand. Nithya giggled, unaware of the weight that word carried.

Soon thereafter, we watched the Tollywood movie RRR. My heart has always leaned towards staying in India. But the spirit of the movie stirred something deeper in me. Its theme of of belonging, courage, and rootedness made the feeling surge with unexpected emotion, reaffirming where I truly wanted to remain.

When we returned to Vuyyuru that evening, joy followed us home.

My grandmother stood at the doorway, her hands quivering as she touched my face. Neighbors gathered, curious, asking questions, listening as Rekha patiently explained what the visa meant.

Later that night, over familiar lentil soup and sweet porridge, and slower conversations, Rekha said softly, “It feels like every road you walked is lighting up again.”

I smiled. “They always were. I just had to walk long enough to find the glow.”

Life returned to balance. Steady and purposeful.

Each morning, the sound of my router connecting felt like possibility renewed. Through that small connection, my keystrokes traveled farther, bridging teams, systems, and lives.

The visa hadn’t changed who I was. It had merely confirmed what I already was. A developer whose work could travel where his eyes could not.

Evenings remained sacred. Rekha describing the changing sky to me. Nithya playing nearby, her laughter echoing in the courtyard.

Sometimes, Rekha would return from the corner shop with two chilled Fantas, just like Rajini madam, who once used to buy them for me during Polytechnic days.

We would sit together on the steps, sipping slowly, letting the day fade into a shared silence that needed no words.

By the end of June 2022, Infosys was ready to send me to the U.S. Everything was aligned.

However, around the same time, a call changed the direction again.

"Hello, Mr. Jannu,"

"We have an opportunity. Would you be open to a discussion?"

I listened, calm and attentive, recognizing that familiar moment when life gently leans forward again.

That evening, I told Rekha about the offer from one of the large finance companies. She listened, then said simply, "Wherever it takes you, we will walk together." We spoke honestly.

Financially, it wouldn't transform everything dramatically. The difference, in reality, was not massive. Two thoughts pulled me back. If something happened there, support would be scarce.
And life in dollars wasn't as simple as it looked from outside.

This wasn't fear. This was clarity. I wasn't running away from the world. I was choosing where I stood strongest.

What many people did not know was that I once carried a very different dream. My ambition was to become a research scientist. I wanted to pursue a PhD and earn the title "Dr" before my name.

It was a pure, innocent hunger of a boy who wanted to reach the furthest edge of what learning could offer. But I realized every step of my education had been sponsored by someone else's kindness. I had promised myself that once I stood on my own feet, my sisters' education would not depend on luck the way mine did.

Dreams are precious, but responsibilities are sacred. And sometimes, choosing family over ambition is its own kind of achievement.

And so, I chose to stay. And I chose to begin again. I joined the firm.

For every interview, every opportunity, there were no special drives. There were no favors and no shortcuts.

I have received calls through job portals like Naukri. The same way thousands of others receive them. Just persistence, preparation, and patience brought me job opportunities.

The boy who once sat in a small blind school in Andhra Pradesh was now being invited to build systems for one of the world's biggest financial giants.

Life hadn't erased its history. It had simply woven everything together again.

Chapter 14: The architecture of sound and logic

When most people begin their careers, they try to fit themselves into the world around them. I began by shaping the world to fit my logic.

From the very first day as a professional, I understood something clearly. I knew my place wasn't in the shifting colors of a user interface but in the deep structural integrity of the backend. The place where logic breathes, decisions are enforced, transactions are trusted, and correctness matters more than appearance.

Over the last 16 years, across telecom, healthcare, and banking, I have lived inside these invisible architectures. Where a sighted developer looks at code and sees indentation, colors, and blocks of text, I experience it differently. I listen to it.

To understand how I work, one must first understand how I read.

I work entirely through JAWS, a screen reader that translates visual interfaces into speech. But reading code is not like reading a novel.

In literature, punctuation can be forgiven. While in software, a missing comma or a misplaced bracket can crash an entire workflow system.

When I navigate a Java class or a Spring Boot configuration file, I don't just hear words. I hear syntax. JAWS reads it out to me in a rapid, mechanical staccato.

"Public class Payment Controller… open brace…"

"If balance greater than zero… open parenthesis…"

"Semicolon. New line."

To an untrained ear, it may sound chaotic. To me, it is music with rules.

I listen at speeds that would sound like gibberish to an untrained ear. From the cadence of speech alone, I build a mental map of indentation levels. I know where a loop begins and ends. Not by seeing the brackets align, but by hearing the logical flow.

I navigate code hierarchy not by scrolling, but by jumping between function definitions and variable declarations using keyboard shortcuts I have memorized over a decade.

The computer doesn't just talk to me, it converses. Every tone is a signal, every pause is a structure.

Because I cannot skim thousands of log lines in seconds, I learned something else early. It is to debug by listening to silence.

I remember a particularly stubborn issue at Wipro. We were working on a partner management system where a scheduler, meant to synchronize metadata across servers, failed silently. Visually, the logs appeared normal. Nothing screamed error.

So I stepped through the execution flow line by line, listening carefully to object states as they evolved. I tracked host identifiers, refresh flags, and database triggers, millisecond by millisecond.

And that is when I heard what was missed. A logical gap where the application context failed to refresh under one specific condition. I did not solve the problem because I was blind. Rather, I solved it because I could not skim. I have to understand every line.

Logic, when listened to carefully, always reveals the truth.

My time at Infosys, from 2013 to 2015 and later from 2019 to 2022, marked a significant transition. I moved from individual problem-solver to conductor of people.

As a Technology Lead, my day revolved around management and delivery. I was responsible for sprint planning, backlog refinement, delivery commitments, and mentoring junior engineers.

I guided juniors not just in fixing issues but in understanding architecture, reading systems, and thinking like engineers who could stand on their own. I designed complex requirements, translated them into clear, buildable components, and implemented them end-to-end every day. That was also my responsibility.

During those years, I also became deeply involved in hiring. I conducted hundreds of interviews for both permanent and contract-based roles. Sitting on interview panels, I learned to listen differently. Without visual cues, I paid attention to tone, pauses, confidence, hesitation, and how answers were structured.

Often, something felt off. A response that sounded memorized. A pause that didn't belong. An explanation that flowed too smoothly without understanding. When I sensed this, I quietly alerted the fellow panel member. More often than not, deeper probing revealed exactly what I had suspected.

It was not intuition alone. It was pattern recognition built through years of careful listening. When you depend on sound, you learn that truth has a rhythm, and inconsistency always breaks it.

Those moments reminded me again that blindness had not limited my judgment. In many ways, it had sharpened it. I was not watching candidates perform; I was listening to who they really were.

During my journey, I broke down complex user stories, guarded timelines, and ensured quality gates like SonarQube stayed green and that Jenkins pipelines flowed without friction.

I became a bridge between client expectations and engineering reality, between pressure and clarity. Success was no longer personal; it was collective.

That phase taught me something invaluable. Leadership is not about visibility but responsibility.

When I joined the large finance company in October 2022 as a Vice President, the flow shifted again.

Here, my role is quieter but heavier. It was less about managing schedules and more about managing complexity. It is a highly specialized, individual contributor role.

As a Lead Software Engineer, I operate deep in architecture. Designing Spring Boot microservices, integrating Kafka for event streaming, and rewriting complex requirements. This work demands solitude, precision, and long attention to detail.

I am responsible for identifying architectural gaps. I don't oversee the code. I inhabit it.

And in that solitude, I found something unexpected. Freedom to go deeper into the technology than ever before.

One challenge, however, remained unresolved for years: system design.

Whiteboarding sessions had always been difficult. Sighted architects drew boxes and arrows; I relied entirely on verbal descriptions. I could hold the entire system clearly in my mind. I knew exactly how the API should talk to the Oracle database. But I couldn't easily 'draw' it for them.

Then came a new ally, Generative AI and Large Language Models (LLMs).

Now, I describe my mental architecture to LLM in plain text. I explain the data flow, service boundaries, and interaction points. Then, I ask the AI to convert my text into PlantUML or Mermaid code. These scripts generate diagrams my team can see.

I send the script to my team, and they see a professional flowchart.

I speak logic. The AI draws the picture.

I review the logic through text. The team reviews it visually.

We are finally looking at the same thing. We are designing from the same mental plane.

This is not convenience. It is liberation.

Ethical AI did not replace my thinking. It gave my thinking a new voice. I am no longer a backend developer who needs help with diagrams; I am an architect who can generate them.

My professional journey has stretched far. From a boy who once struggled to find accessible textbooks to a Vice President designing enterprise systems for a global bank.

My work evolved from system development at Infosys to leading complex platforms at the large finance company. From cassette tapes to JAWS and now Generative AI; the tools have evolved, but the core remains the same.

Software does not ask whether you can see the screen. It asks whether your logic holds.

That has always been my strength and my comfort.

And yet, just as I mastered this new mode of work, life presented a challenge that code could not solve. A battle that was physical, painful, and personal was waiting just ahead.

In late 2022, life reminded me that stability is never permanent.

It was 28th November, 2022, nearly midnight. The city outside slept while my screen still glowed with meeting notes and silent notifications. As I prepared to shut down, my phone rang.

The voice on the other end shuddered, “Nani, your grandmother is critical. She is admitted to a hospital near Vijayawada.”

The words felt distant at first, unreal. Then instinct took over it. By dawn, I was on a train heading south. The wind rushed through open windows. The scent of wet fields rose through the morning haze.

Those miles going back carried memory. And every minute carried prayer.

At the hospital, the air smelled of rain and disinfectant. Machines beeped slowly. She lay still, fragile, oxygen tubes tracing delicate lines across her face. I took her hand in mine, “Ammamma, it’s me. Nani.”

Her fingers moved faintly. A whisper of recognition. Her touch carried a lifetime of love.

By evening, when we all were praying in the corridors of the hospital, the doctor came quietly. "We tried our best," he said. "She is no more."

The words did not crash. They settled heavily. Rekha held my arm. Nithya clung to Rekha's saree, sensing grief she couldn't yet name. And I stood there, hearing nothing but my heartbeat.

That night, we travelled back to Vuyyuru with her. The road felt impossibly long. Every turn echoed her voice, her laughter, and her prayers before every exam and interview of my life.

At home, incense mixed with the smell of damp soil. Neighbors gathered in quiet solidarity. Rituals began. Chants rose softly into the air.

I touched her forehead one last time and whispered, "You never let go of my hand, Ammamma. I'll keep holding yours, just differently now."

For the first time, silence of my grandmother felt heavier than blindness.

Returning to work was harder than I expected. Screens, code, and calls felt distant. But slowly, things get back on track. And I knew even my grandmother would have wanted that way.

In every smooth deployment, in every bug resolved, I felt her presence. The woman who taught me patience long before the world taught me logic.

Sometimes, late at night, when a final build compiled successfully, I would whisper softly, "Build complete, Ammamma." And I could sense her saying, "I know you will complete it, Nani."

Many people supported me constantly throughout my journey. But my grandmother's presence in my life was something that I cannot express but feel.

Chapter 15: The light within

For a while, life had finally found its pace again.

My workplace flowed with purpose. Structured, challenging, and deeply fulfilling. At home, Rekha and little Nithya filled every quiet corner with warmth.

After years of climbing walls and breaking barriers, my days had settled into a balance. Calm mornings, meaningful work, and peaceful evenings. It felt like life had finally exhaled.

But life has its own language and it rarely announces the next storm. Sometimes, it arrives silently, slipping into the edge of peace long before you notice its shadow.

Around April 2023, a dull ache began in my lower back. A small tug at first, which I dismissed as the cost of long hours of work.

But each day sharpened it. Soon the pain traveled down my spine, through my legs, until even turning in bed felt like fire slicing through bone.

Rekha noticed before I admitted it. "You're straining yourself too much, Nani," she whispered, massaging warm oil onto my back.

I said what most people say when they want to protect the ones they love. "It's nothing."

But by May, even small movements felt like dragging the weight of the world. The MRI scans finally spoke what I didn't want to hear.

The doctor's voice was steady, almost too calm. "Severe disc collapse between L3 and L4. Spinal fusion is the only permanent solution."

Silence filled the room. This time the enemy wasn't a system, a rulebook, or prejudice. The enemy was inside my own body.

I then visited multiple doctors. Among them were Dr. Shekhar Reddy and Dr. B. G. Rathnam. The actual diagnosis was done by Dr. B. G. Rathnam at Apollo for back pain in June 2023. Both of their support in recovery and operation was commendable, which helped me recover sooner than usual.

From the moment surgery was mentioned, Pooja entered our lives like a steady flame. She came as a nurse. And stayed as a family member.

She moved into our home, carrying with her a discipline so gentle that our house's routine changed without effort.

At dawn, her soft footsteps signaled medicines being arranged. By noon, I heard the rattle of spoons as she prepared warm soups. Evenings brought the scent of antiseptic blending with the aroma of Rekha's cooking.

I woke in the darkest hours and used to see Pooja adjusting my pillows or checking my breathing.

"It's okay, sir. Go back to sleep," she whispered.

When salary was delayed due to my medical expenses, she didn't mention it, not even in passing.

"Sir, I'm here for your recovery. Payment can wait."

Her presence restored something illness tried to steal. Dignity.

The day of the surgery at Apollo Hospitals arrived wrapped in sterile stillness. I could smell antiseptic and cold metal from the surroundings.

Rekha walked beside my stretcher, her grip firm, her silence stronger than any words she could have spoken.

Inside the operating theater, the word shifted into sound. Gloves snapping on, monitors beeping.

An oxygen mask descended. My world narrowed to breathing and fading voices.

When consciousness returned, pain was waiting for me. It was raw and merciless. Through the haze, one voice pierced the chaos. “It’s okay, sir. Just breathe. You’re safe.”

Pooja. She held my hand the entire night. A lighthouse in a storm I couldn’t see.

“You’ll walk again, sir. Just not tonight.”

That night felt endless, but compassion made it bearable.

Recovery was not a journey. It was a crawl. Sitting up took days, turning in bed required strategy. Every inch felt like fighting gravity itself. Those days, my brother-in-law Manoj and Sridhar supported me a lot, in every way he could.

Rekha and Pooja became my anchors, adjusting blankets, feeding me spoon by spoon, and whispering hope into the cracks of my fear. “You’ll heal, Nani. Just a little longer.”

Pooja’s discipline stitched each day together. Medicines, wound dressings, physiotherapy.

“Each step is progress, sir. Don’t measure time, measure courage.”

Medical bills piled up, threatening to collapse everything we had built. But as I often told myself, “Money can be rebuilt. Life cannot.”

My uncle Durgarao and my brother-in-law Rambabu visited me often to check on me, though my father didn’t.

By October 2023, I could finally stand again. Slowly, painfully, but upright. A victory only the body understands.

I thought the worst had passed. But the body carries its own mysteries.

It was 9th August 2024. That morning in the office felt ordinary. Cool air, light chatter, and the distant noise of systems.

But something inside me felt off. A strange heaviness in my limbs, an unfamiliar fatigue.

I walked to the medical bay. The nurse checked my vitals and then asked me to rest. As I lay down on the bed, there was a buzz of the air conditioner blended with distant office chatter.

Then suddenly, my arm jerked. Again and again. My entire body convulsed uncontrollably. The bed shook. Equipment fell. Voices rose.

I heard my manager's urgent, steady voice above the panic: "Stay with us, Nagababu. We're getting you to Apollo right now."

The stretcher wheels rolled fast. The ambulance tore through traffic. A blur of sirens and fear.

In that moment, my world shrank to a single, trembling prayer, "Please… not again."

Days faded into tests, needles, and consultations. Finally, the doctors named the enemy, myoclonus. It is a rare neurological disorder that triggers involuntary muscle jerks. No clear cause. No guaranteed cure.

It was during this phase that Sneha, my physiotherapist, became another unexpected turning point. I had reached out to her when the pain felt unmanageable. After observing me closely, she suggested that I consult an endocrinologist, sending that something deeper might play.

She connected me to Dr. Abhinananda, who in turn referred me to Dr. Suresh Babu at Arete Hospital. The chain of intuition, care, and timely guidance changed the course of my recovery. Under Dr. Suresh Babu's treatment, things slowly began to stabilize. Not dramatically, not overnight, but enough for me to breathe again.

Those days were relentless. Most times, it was just Pooja and me making hospital visits back and forth. Rekha stayed home with Nithya, managing school mornings, meals, and the quiet worries of a child who sensed that something was wrong. Only after sending Nithya to school would Rekha come rushing to the hospital, carrying exhaustion she never spoke about.

We lived in shifts of strength, handing it to one another when one of us ran out.

Between August and December 2024, I was hospitalized four times. Three times at Apollo Jubilee Hills and one time at Arete Hospitals, Hyderabad. Every stay at the hospital was a small war fought inch by inch.

The jerks came like waves. Sometimes soft, sometimes violent enough to throw my body balance off. Sleep deserted me. Peace, a memory.

Rekha stood firm and remained my shield. Her voice steady even when exhaustion pulled at its edges. “You’ve come through worse, Nani. You’ll come through this too.”

Nithya would visit and press her tiny hand into mine.

“Nanna, I’ll take you home soon.”

In that small touch lived more medicine than the IV lines running into my veins.

And through it all, Pooja stood like a wall. Coordinating with doctors. Managing medicines. Holding my world when I couldn’t.

“Sir, pain can’t stop you. You are stronger than it.”

Even when months of her salary were pending, she refused to leave. She stayed, not as a nurse but as grace given form.

Some people perform their duty. Some become a blessing. She was both. These months taught me a new kind of surrender. Doctors adjusted dosages. I adjusted expectations.

Some days, I prayed for healing. Other days, I prayed simply for rest.

Financial strain deepened. But help arrived from unexpected corners. Friends, colleagues, and relatives stepped forward, easing the weight of uncertainty. The prime supporters throughout were Pavan, Sudhir, and my uncle Durgarao. Their support was proof that faith doesn't erase suffering. It carries you through it.

Faith is not always loud. Sometimes it is the strength to breathe through one more night.

Something shifted by mid-November 2024.

The jerks softened. Nights grew calmer. One morning, I realized I had slept for three straight hours. A miracle disguised as rest.

Rekha's voice carried renewed hope.

"See, you're getting better, Nani."

By the end of the month, I could sit up, type, and even take on small tasks.

When my laptop booted and JAWS said, “Welcome to Windows.”

I smiled and whispered back, “Welcome back, Nagababu.”

It wasn’t just the system restarting. It was my life. The pain still lingers, quiet but constant. A shadow that walks beside me. But I have stopped fighting it. Now, I walk with it. Because pain, too, is a proof of survival.

7 January, 2025. This day became one of those strange days when life places joy and grief in the same frame.

By then, I had started working from home in early December. The steroids kept my body stable, though my strength was still returning. The next day, I was supposed to resume office after months of battling jerks and fear.

That morning, I attended a felicitation ceremony where the Governor of Telangana honored individuals for their contributions. It was on the occasion of Louis Braille's birthday. I stood there, humbled, holding the moment like a silent victory after a long war. A photograph was taken, capturing what looked like confidence but was really gratitude.

In the same hall, amid applause and formal speeches, I met an old schoolmate from Devnar. We shared memories, laughter, and updates. And then, almost gently, he said something I never expected.

"Did you hear, Nani? Anasurya teacher passed away."

For a moment, the world around me blurred into silence. She was one of the earliest guiding lights in my life. A woman who had shown my mother how to navigate the world, who had taken care of me like her own child.

Standing there in a hall filled with celebration, I felt the weight of her absence.

Life has a way of reminding us that every step forward carries shadows of those who shaped us.

Just when I thought life had paused its trials, another unexpected turn appeared. It was without drama, just the way real challenges often appear.

In early 2025, my routine medical check led to a suggestion for thyroid surgery. The doctors were not alarmed, but something inside me hesitated. I postponed it, telling myself it could wait.

But on November 10, during a follow-up at Apollo Hospital, the moment the ultrasound probe touched my neck, I sensed concern in the room. The technician's silence felt heavier than words.

I consulted Dr. Siddharth Chakravarthy, Consultant Robotic Endocrine and Breast Onco Surgeon, Apollo Hospital, Jubilee Hills. He did not waste a moment. "We must do an FNAC immediately," he said.

The next day, when the report arrived, I was at home with Pooja. The others had gone to a marriage. The result confirmed what I feared. It was cancer.

For a moment, the room felt still. Not dark. Not broken. Just still. As if life was giving me space to absorb the truth. The doctor said it should be operated on soon.

Pooja accompanied me for the procedure. Rekha and her cousin Navya were with me during hospitalization.

In mid-November, my thyroid gland was removed. The surgery went smoothly and gave me a sense of relief. Not because the danger was gone, but because the uncertainty was.

I didn't want to trouble my mother with worry, so I told her almost 15 days after the surgery. She held her breath and said only one line, "Your courage will save you."

In the coming months, radioactive treatment is planned. And the doctor suggested that checkups should follow once every six months. That path ahead was clear, even if it wasn't easy.

This incident taught me something precise and personal. I learned that uncertainty is often heavier than pain itself. Strength, I realized, is not the absence of fear. It is the discipline of moving forward while fear walks quietly beside you.

I have walked blind into every chapter of my life, yet I have never walked without courage. This is no different.

My life has been a series of storms. Blindness, poverty, rejection, surgery, neurological battles. Each storm trying to drown me, each storm teaching me breathe deeper.

But every storm left something behind. Wisdom, humility, courage, and light. I have learned that pain does not define you, endurance does.

And endurance is never solitary. It is built by hands that lift you when you fall.

Rekha's tireless patience, Nithya's innocence, Pooja's unwavering compassion, and the unexpected kindness of friends and strangers. They are my light, not the kind you see shining from outside, but the kind that refuses to go out.

Life wove many people into my journey, each in their own way. But some threads never loosened. Pavan was one of them. Steady through every phase, never stepping away. Some friendships are not measured by words or milestones; they are measured by presence. Through every stage of my life, Pavan remained the same.

Even now, when pain whispers from old wounds, I remind myself, "You've walked through darkness before, Nagababu. You'll always find your way back to light."

Because light, I've learned, isn't something you see. It's something you carry.

Chapter 16: The Architecture of My Learning

There are two kinds of light in this world. One that enters through the eyes, and one that rises quietly from within. I grew up guided by the second one. The kind that doesn't dim with darkness, the kind that whispers through sound, touch, memory, and imagination.

People often ask how I study, write, or code without sight. To them, it feels extraordinary. To me, it is simply the architecture of my life. A structure built not on vision, but on curiosity, persistence, and evolving technology that learned to speak my language.

This chapter is that unseen journey, where Braille gave me roots, audio gave me endurance, JAWS gave me wings, and generative AI finally gave me a way to 'see.'

The origin of Braille - The light behind the dots

Before my story comes the story of the boy who changed all our stories. Louis Braille, blinded at age three, lived in a world that offered the blind neither books nor dignity. At 15, he created a miracle, a system of raised dots inspired by soldiers reading messages in the dark.

He didn't just create a script. He created access. He created identity. He created equality through touch.

Every time my fingers glide across raised dots, I feel him beside me. A reminder that determination from one lifetime can illuminate another.

Phase 1: The mechanics of 6 Braille dots

I met Braille before I met language. While other children saw the alphabet, I learned to feel it.

Braille is not a language. It is a code, a tiny 6-dot cell that transforms into alphabets, punctuation, mathematics, and even music.

- Dot 1 is top-left
- Dot 6 is bottom-right
- A = Dot 1
- B = Dots 1-2

- C = Dots 1-4

Each combination becomes a character. Simple. Precise. Infinite.

Reading Braille is one skill. Writing is another battlefield.

Using a slate and stylus, we punch dots from the backwards, right to left, so that when the paper is flipped, the text reads correctly.

Tap… tap… tap…

That metallic rhythm was my childhood, discipline made audible.

Braille gave me literacy, but it wasn't light. When my classmates carried a book, I carried a stack of ten. A single subject could fill entire volumes.

But weight was not the real challenge, scarcity was. In the 90s, there were barely any Braille presses. Sometimes, an entire school had just one copy of a textbook. Each one of us took less time to study because we had to pass it to another student. Higher-class books didn't exist at all.

So we improvised. Someone read aloud while I punched notes at full speed. Breathlessly capturing borrowed knowledge.

Sometimes my fingers went numb from tracing worn dots. Sometimes books flattened inside bags and erased words forever.

Braille taught me literacy. It also taught me resilience.

Phase 2: The audio cassette bridge

When Braille reached its limit, sound became my second teacher. This hiss of a cassette player filled my evenings.

Volunteers, teachers, and friends recorded lessons line by line. But tapes were fragile. They snapped, snarled, stretched, and distorted the truth.

Searching for a topic meant rewinding and fast-forwarding blindly through a reel of magnetic tape. Yet I persisted.

Braille gave me the foundation. Audio cassettes gave me perseverance.

Phase 3: Digital awakening with JAWS

Everything changed in 9th standard. The day I heard a computer speak, my world divided into before and after. It was a revelation.

JAWS (Job Access With Speech) converted the entire screen into sound. But understanding it requires a different way of thinking. While a sighted person can see menus, icons, errors, and everything at one glance.

For me, JAWS reads it top to bottom, line by line, which is the Straw effect. Like reading a newspaper through a narrow straw. To cope, I learned to crank the speaking speed higher and higher until the voice became a high-speed blur of data. Unintelligible to me, but clear to me.

Before JAWS, I wanted for someone to read to me.

After JAWS, I could read at 2 a.m. and even feed a document into the system.

It was the first taste of true digital independence.

Phase 4: The hardware evolution

As the world evolved, so did I. From polytechnic to engineering. The transition of storage changed and the world shed its weight.

- Floppy disks made me nervous, as one magnet could erase everything.
- CDs and flash drives felt like miracles as I carried entire books in my pocket.
- The Internet and cloud felt like stepping into a borderless, infinite library.

For the first time, learning was not limited by scarcity. Information became fluid, portable, and on-demand.

Technology didn't just support me, it carried me.

Phase 5: AI becomes my vision

Even after decades of progress, one barrier remained unbreakable. Images.

JAWS could read text, but for every diagram it said one thing, "Graphic."

Architecture diagrams, flowcharts, and screenshots, all of these were locked doors. I could code the logic but couldn't see the design.

Then came generative AI and large language models. Suddenly, the world opened.

To describe the visual, I upload a complex architecture diagram and ask, “Describe the data flow.”

AI analyzes the arrows and boxes and explains, “The User API connects to the Oracle Database, which then syncs with the Kafka stream.” In seconds, the invisible becomes visible through words.

To create the visual, I describe a system in plain English.

User hits API → Service → Oracle DB → Kakfa event

AI generates the Mermaid or PlantUML code. Now my team and I “see” the same architecture. They visually, I textually.

AI didn’t just help me work. It erased the last major barrier between me and the visual world.

The unseen barrier, when code itself becomes blind

I must be honest, technology is only as good as the humans who build it.

Despite everything, I still face digital walls daily. One of the greatest barriers is inaccessible design.

A sighted person sees a “Buy Now” button. I hear “Button 12,” “Unlabeled graphic,” or “Click here.”

Click here? Why? For what? Dynamic websites update visually without telling the screen reader. You see flashing urgency. I hear silence.

Technology evolved, yes. But accessibility often lags behind intention.

A note to developers: Code with inclusion at its core

If you write code, you can change my world. Accessibility is not expensive. It is empathy translated to HTML.

Here is how you can help:

- Label buttons: Code it as <button aria-label="Meaning full label">. That tiny tag tells my ears what your eyes see.
- Use headings: Use <h1>, <h2> tags. They allow me to skim a page by jumping between sections instead of listening to every word.
- Describe images: Don't let the Alt Text say "Image." Write meaningful Alt Text.
- Keyboard test: If you can't use your site with just the Tab key, neither can I.

Accessibility is not charity. It is good engineering.

Moments from my journey

Fig 1: My first birthday in Vuyyuru on 8th June 1987.

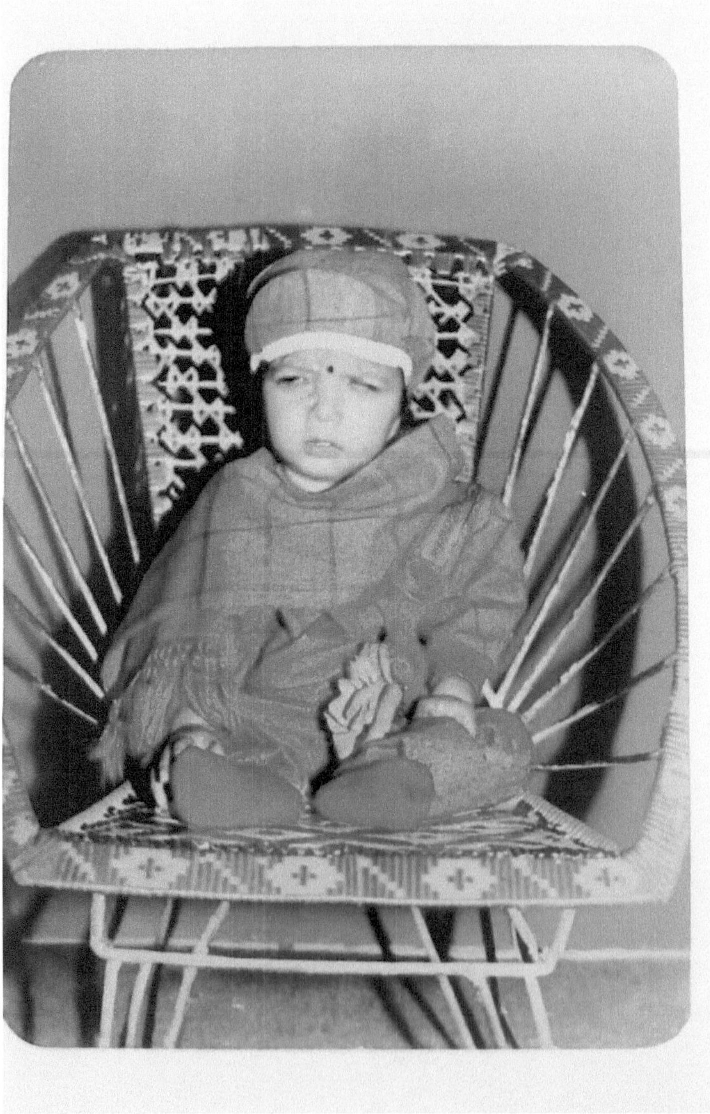

Fig 2: Braille slate and stylus

Fig 3: Taylor's frame

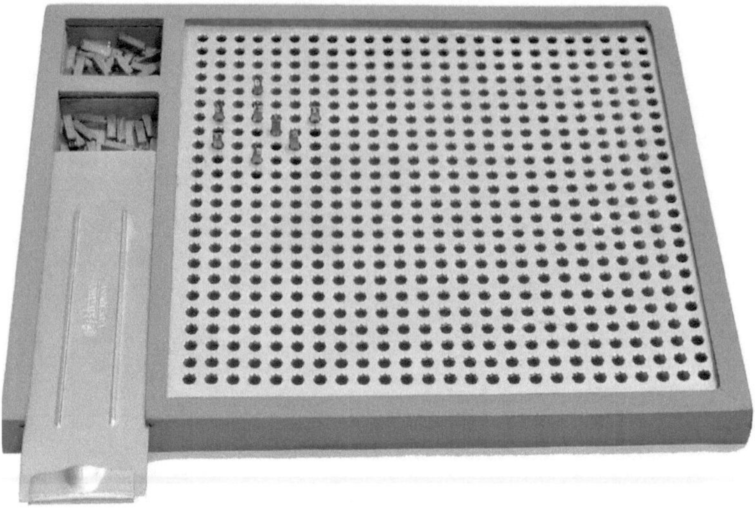

Fig 4: At Devnar School for the Blind, March 2000, receiving my prize during the annual day celebrations.

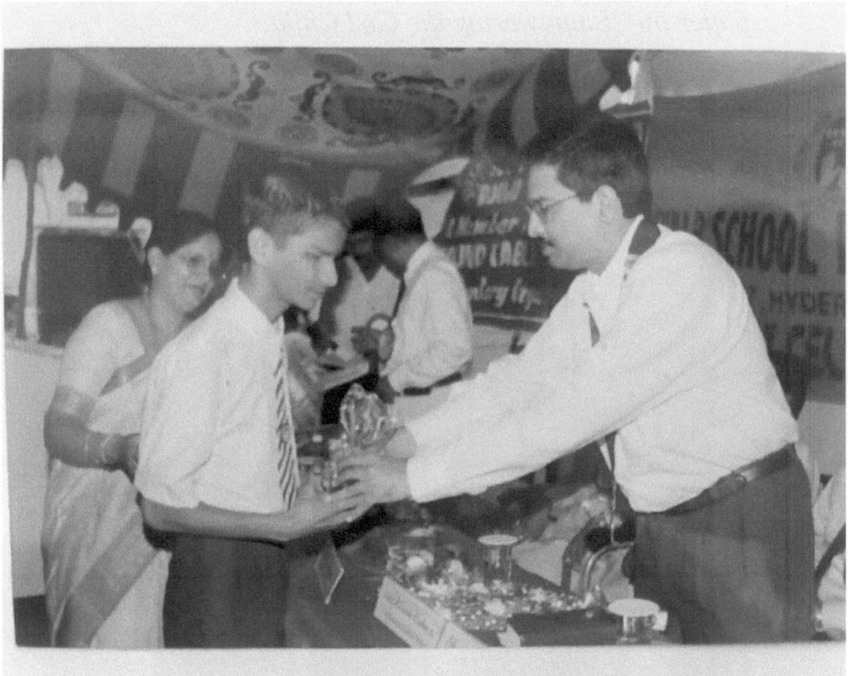

Fig 5: Won the national-level first prize on 4th November, 2004, at the National ISTE convention for submitting my paper on "Empowering the Girl Child."

Fig 6: Chessboard for the blind

Fig 7: Wedding day on 2nd April, 2010, in Hyderabad.

Fig 8: Arya Samaj wedding on 13th April, 2010.

Fig 9: Felicitation by the Governor of Telangana on the 216th birthday of Louis Braille in January 2025 at Raj Bhavan.

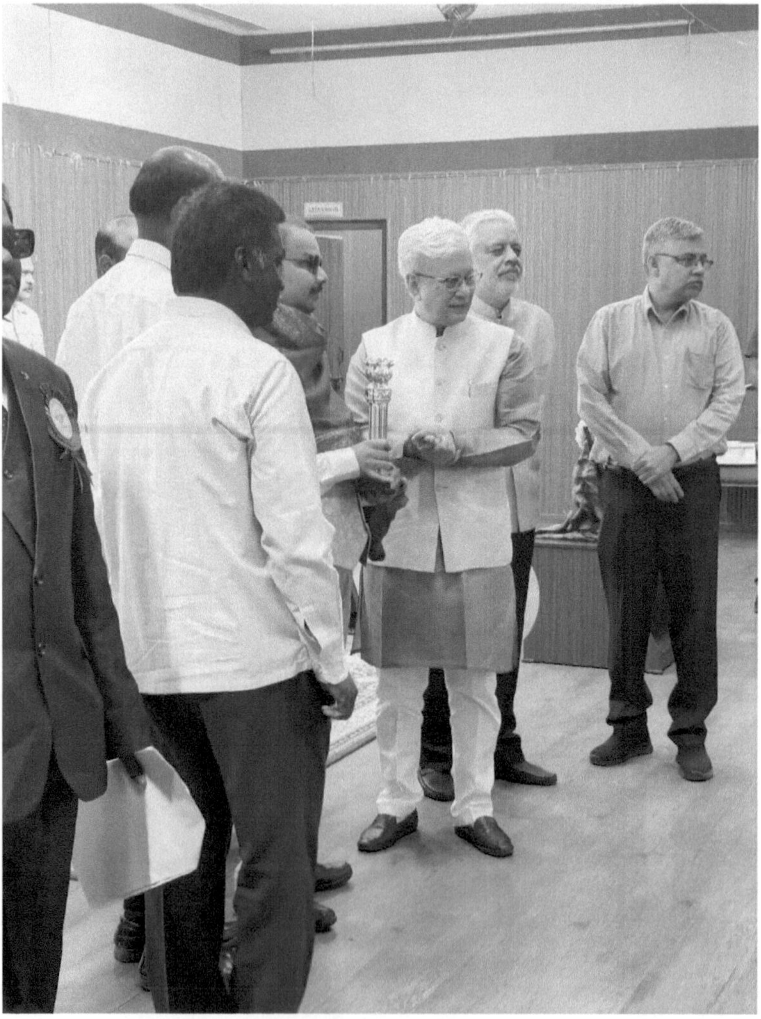

Fig 10: On 17th February 2024, at SR Gudlavalleru Engineering College, I was honored with the GEC Ratna Award in the category of Other Walks of Life during the Silver Jubilee celebrations.

Fig 11: Won a National Award from the Indian Society of Technical Education (ISTE), Gujarat, for presenting a research paper on "Girl Empowerment."

బహుమతి అందుకుంటున్న జన్ను నాగబాబు

అంధ విద్యార్థికి జాతీయ బహుమతి

గుడ్లవల్లేరు, నవంబరు 15 (న్యూస్‌టుడే): జాతీయ సాంకేతిక విద్యాసదస్సులో స్థానిక పాలిటెక్నిక్ కళాశాలకు చెందిన అంధవిద్యార్థి జాతీయ ప్రథమబహుమతిని సాధించగా, మరో ముగ్గురు బహుమతులు పొందారు. దేశవ్యాప్తంగా సాంకేతిక విద్యావ్యవస్థను నియంత్రించే కీలకమైన ఎ.ఐ.సి.టి.ఇ.కి అనుబంధంగా సాంకేతిక విద్యావిధానాల రూపకల్పనలో ప్రథమపాత్ర వహించే ఇండియన్ సొసైటీ ఫర్ టెక్నికల్ ఎడ్యుకేషన్(ఐఎస్‌టిఇ) ప్రతి సంవత్సరం ఒక్కో రాష్ట్రంలో జాతీయ సదస్సులు నిర్వహిస్తుంది. దీనిలోభాగంగా ఇటీవల 7వ ఐ.ఎస్.టి.ఇ. జాతీయసదస్సును గుజరాత్ ఆనంద్‌లోని వల్లభ విద్యానగర్‌లో నిర్వహించారు. దీనిలో స్థానిక ఎ.ఎ.ఎన్.ఎం. మరియు వి.వి.ఆర్.ఎస్.ఆర్. పాలిటెక్నిక్ కళాశాల విద్యార్థులు ఎనిమిది మంది పాల్గొని రెండు జాతీయ ప్రథమ, రెండు తృతీయ బహుమతులు సాధించారు. బాలికా సాధికారిత అనే అంశంపై అధ్యయన పత్రాలు సమర్పించిన కంప్యూటర్ చివరి సంవత్సరం చదివే అంధవిద్యార్థి జన్ను నాగబాబు జాతీయ ప్రథమబహుమతిని సాధించాడు. 'గ్లోబల్ సిస్టమ్ ఫర్ మొబైల్ కమ్యూనికేషన్' అనే అంశంపై ఎలక్ట్రానిక్స్ చివరి సంవత్సరం విద్యార్థి డి.మోహన్‌నరేంద్ర జాతీయ ప్రథమ బహుమతిని పొందారు. 'మైక్రోవేవ్ రేడియేషన్ ఫ్రమ్ మొబైల్‌ఫోన్' అనే అంశంలో కంప్యూటర్ చివరి సంవత్సరం విద్యార్థి ఎం.వర్మ, ఎం.ప్రసాద్ తృతీయ బహుమతులు సాధించారు. స్థానిక ఐ.ఎస్.టి.ఇ స్టూడెంట్స్ చాప్టర్ సలహాదారు ఎన్.శ్రీనివాసమూర్తి ఆధ్వర్యంలో విద్యార్థులకు శిక్షణ ఇచ్చిన అధ్యాపకులు శంకరరావు, పి.రజని తదితరులను కళాశాల ప్రిన్సిపాల్ సిహెచ్. వెంకట్రామన్న, సిబ్బంది అభినందించారు.

Fig 12: This newspaper article highlights my journey as a visually impaired student pursuing technical education.

లక్ష్యం, తపన, కసి ఈ మూడు తోడైతే ! ?

డీలర్లు కావలెను
Cell : 9848396534
HAIR OIL
OMIN LOCKETS
OMIN GKS Products (Regd.), Dr. SHAIK SHAFIUDDIN
TADPATRI

వండర్ వరల్డ్ మార్చి 2004

13

Fig 13: Writing 1st year Polytechnic exams with the help of a scribe.

పాలిటెక్నిక్ పరీక్షలు రాస్తున్న అంధ విద్యార్థి

గుడ్లవల్లేరు, ఏప్రిల్ 4 (న్యూస్‌టుడే): రాష్ట్ర సాంకేతిక విద్యాశాఖ చరిత్రలోనే తొలిసారిగా ఉయ్యూరు గ్రామానికి చెందిన జన్ను నాగబాబు(17) అనే అంధ యువకుడు గుడ్లవల్లేరులోని స్థానిక ఎ.ఎ.ఎస్.ఎం. అండ్ వి.వి.ఆర్.ఎస్.ఆర్. పాలిటెక్నిక్ కాలేజీలో ప్రథమ సంవత్సరం పాలిటెక్నిక్ కంప్యూటర్ (డి.సి.ఎం.ఇ) పరీక్షలు రాస్తున్నాడు. మార్చి 24వ తేదీ నుంచి ప్రారంభమైన మొదటి సంవత్సరం పాలిటెక్నిక్ కంప్యూటర్ విభాగం పరీక్షలను నాగబాబు బోర్డు ప్రత్యేక అనుమతితో సహాయకుడి సాయంతో పరీక్షలు రాస్తున్నాడు. నాగబాబు అంధుడైనా చదువులో మంచి ప్రతిభ చూపుతున్నట్లు కంప్యూటర్ విభాగం హెడ్ ఎం.శంకరరావు, ఇన్‌స్ట్రక్టర్ పి.రజనిలు తెలిపారు. ఇప్పటి వరకు పరీక్షలు సంతృప్తికరంగా రాసినట్లు నాగబాబు తెలిపారు.

సహాయకుడు(స్క్రైబ్) సహాయంతో పరీక్షలు రాస్తున్న నాగబాబు

చూపు లేదు.. కానీ దీక్షా తీక్షణత ఉంది

నాగబాబుపై ప్రత్యేక వార్త - నేటి వసుంధర ||| లో

Fig 14: This article highlights my struggles and achievements as the first 100% blind polytechnic graduate to appear for ECET. Pavan followed the same path 2 years later.

పరీక్షల్లో అంధ విద్యార్థుల విజయం

గుడ్లవల్లేరు, జూన్ 5 (న్యూస్‌టుడే): స్థానిక ఏ.ఏ.ఎన్.ఎం. అండ్ వి.వి.ఆర్.ఎస్.ఆర్ పాలిటెక్నిక్ కళాశాల అంధ విద్యార్థి జన్ను నాగబాబు (ఉయ్యూరు) ఏప్రిల్లో రాసిన తృతీయ సంవత్సర పరీక్షల్లో ప్రథమశ్రేణిలో ఉత్తీర్ణుడయ్యాడు. రాష్ట్ర సాంకేతిక విద్యాశాఖ చరిత్రలో పాలిటెక్నిక్ విద్యను పూర్తిచేసిన తొలి అంధ(నూరు-శాతం) విద్యార్థిగా రికార్డు సృష్టించాడు. ఇదే కళాశాలలో ప్రథమ సంవత్సరం కంప్యూటర్ విద్యను అభ్యసించే మరో అంధ విద్యార్థి లింగం పవన్‌కుమార్ (ఉయ్యూరు) సైతం మొదటి సంవత్సరం ఫలితాలలో 86.1 శాతం ఉత్తీర్ణత సాధించాడు. ఇలా వీరిరువురికి సాంకేతిక విద్యను బోధించిన కళాశాలగా స్థానిక పాలిటెక్నిక్ కళాశాల సుస్థిర స్థానాన్ని పొందింది.

అంధుడైనా ఆగని అక్షర యజ్ఞం

పుట్టుకతోనే అంధుడైన నాగబాబు 2002లో పాలిటెక్నిక్ ప్రవేశపరీక్ష రాసి గుడ్లవల్లేరు పాలిటెక్నిక్ కళాశాలలో కంప్యూటర్ విభాగం (డి.సి.ఎం.ఇ) విద్యార్థిగా అడుగుపెట్టాడు. పట్టుదలతో చదివి ప్రథమ సంవత్సరంలో 59.44, ద్వితీయలో 72.66, తృతీయ సంవత్సరంలో 76.02 శాతం మార్కులతో ఉత్తీర్ణుడయ్యాడు. నిరుపేద కావడంతో రూ. 21 వేల ఫీజును కళాశాల యాజమాన్యం కట్టించుకోక ఉదారతను చాటుకుంది. బీటెక్ పూర్తి చేసి సాఫ్ట్‌వేర్ ఇంజినీర్‌గా స్థిరపడాలన్నదే తన ధ్యేయమని, దీనికై నేడు తొలిమెట్టు ఎక్కానని నాగబాబు పేర్కొన్నాడు.

ఈసెట్ ఫలితంపై న్యాయపోరాటం

ఇంజినీరింగ్ విద్యాభ్యాసానికై నాగబాబు న్యాయపోరాటం సాగిస్తున్నాడు. కళాశాల యాజమాన్యం ఇంజినీరింగ్ ప్రవేశ పరీక్షకై ఉచిత శిక్షణను ఇప్పించగా ఈసెట్ ప్రవేశ పరీక్షకు దరఖాస్తు చేసుకున్నాడు. పరీక్ష ముందురోజు జె.ఎన్.టి.యు.ను సహాయకుడి కోసం 'కోరగా' అధికారులు అసలు పరీక్ష రాయడానికి వీలులేదని అభ్యంతరం చెప్పారు. దీనిపై హైకోర్టులో అదేరోజు ప్రత్యేక రిట్ వేయగా పరీక్ష రాయించాలని తీర్పు రావడంతో మే 4న హైదరాబాద్‌లో ఈసెట్ పరీక్ష రాశాడు. మే 11న విడుదలైన ఫలితాలలో అతని ఫలితాన్ని ప్రకటించకుండా నిలుపుదల చేశారు. దీనిపై సోమవారం హైకోర్టులో రిట్ దాఖలు చేయనున్నట్లు వెల్లడించాడు.

Fig 15: This article recorded my journey as a blind student who refused to let vision define learning.

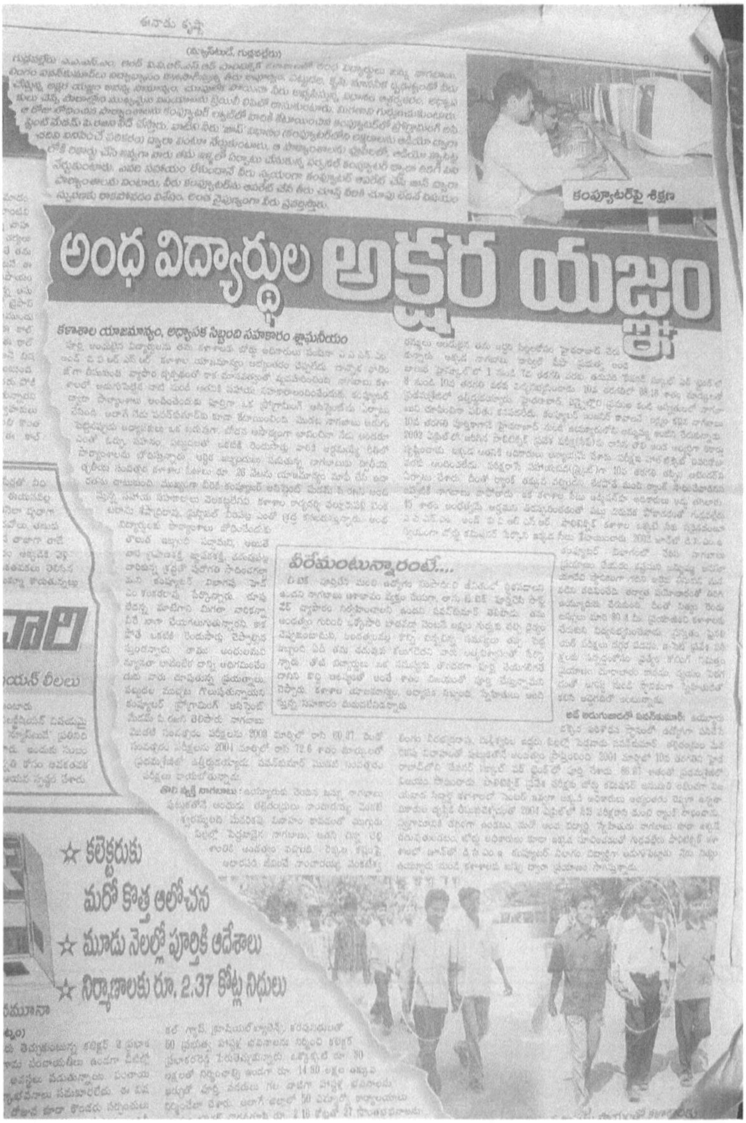

కంప్యూటర్‌పై శిక్షణ

అంధ విద్యార్థుల అక్షర యజ్ఞం

కళాశాల యాజమాన్యం, అధ్యాపక సిబ్బంది సహకారం శ్లాఘనీయం

వీరేమంటున్నారంటే....

☆ కలెక్టరుకు మరో కొత్త ఆలోచన

☆ మూడు నెలల్లో పూర్తికి ఆదేశాలు

☆ నిర్మాణాలకు రూ. 2.37 కోట్ల నిధులు

Fig 16: This article records a first in the state, my admission as a blind student to Gudlavalleru Engineering College.

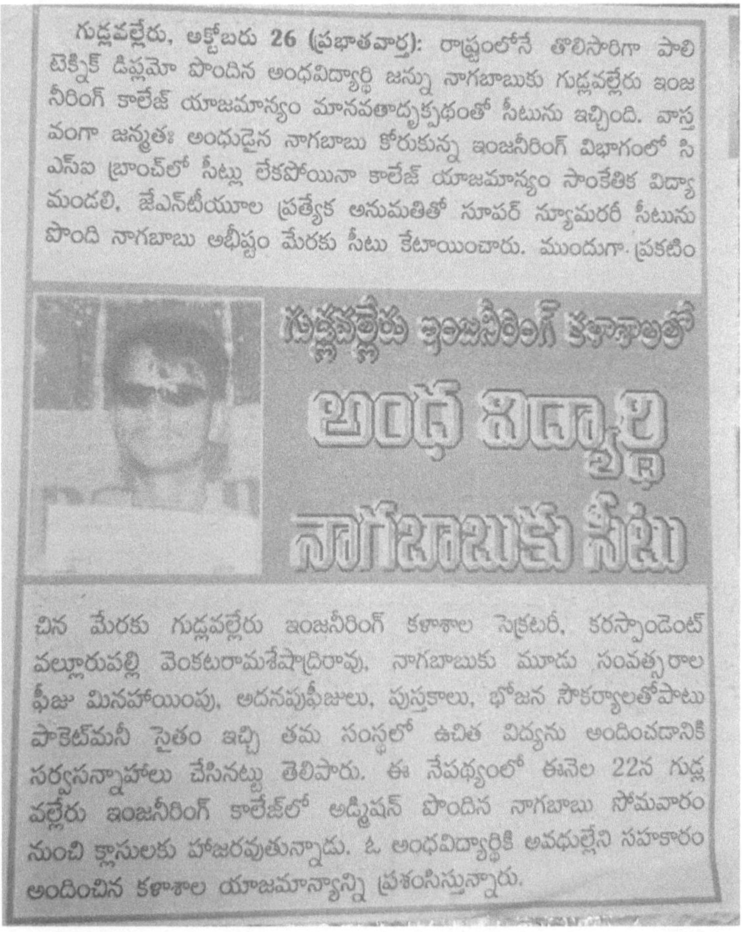

గుడ్లవల్లేరు ఇంజనీరింగ్ కళాశాలలో

అంధ విద్యార్థి నాగబాబుకు సీటు

గుడ్లవల్లేరు, అక్టోబరు 26 (ప్రభాతవార్త): రాష్ట్రంలోనే తొలిసారిగా పాలిటెక్నిక్ డిప్లమో పొందిన అంధవిద్యార్థి జన్ను నాగబాబుకు గుడ్లవల్లేరు ఇంజనీరింగ్ కాలేజ్ యాజమాన్యం మానవతాదృక్పథంతో సీటును ఇచ్చింది. వాస్తవంగా జన్మతః అంధుడైన నాగబాబు కోరుకున్న ఇంజనీరింగ్ విభాగంలో సిఎస్ఐ బ్రాంచ్‌లో సీట్లు లేకపోయినా కాలేజ్ యాజమాన్యం సాంకేతిక విద్యా మండలి, జేఎన్‌టీయూల ప్రత్యేక అనుమతితో సూపర్ న్యూమరరీ సీటును పొంది నాగబాబు అభీష్టం మేరకు సీటు కేటాయించారు. ముందుగా ప్రకటించిన మేరకు గుడ్లవల్లేరు ఇంజనీరింగ్ కళాశాల సెక్రటరీ, కరస్పాండెంట్ వల్లూరుపల్లి వెంకటరామశేషాద్రిరావు, నాగబాబుకు మూడు సంవత్సరాల ఫీజు మినహాయింపు, అదనపుఫీజులు, పుస్తకాలు, భోజన సౌకర్యాలతోపాటు పాకెట్‌మనీ సైతం ఇచ్చి తమ సంస్థలో ఉచిత విద్యను అందించడానికి సర్వసన్నాహాలు చేసినట్లు తెలిపారు. ఈ నేపథ్యంలో ఈనెల 22న గుడ్లవల్లేరు ఇంజనీరింగ్ కాలేజ్‌లో అడ్మిషన్ పొందిన నాగబాబు సోమవారం నుంచి క్లాసులకు హాజరవుతున్నాడు. ఓ అంధవిద్యార్థికి అవధుల్లేని సహకారం అందించిన కళాశాల యాజమాన్యాన్ని ప్రశంసిస్తున్నారు.

Fig 17: This article tells my story as the first blind student to study in an Engineering College.

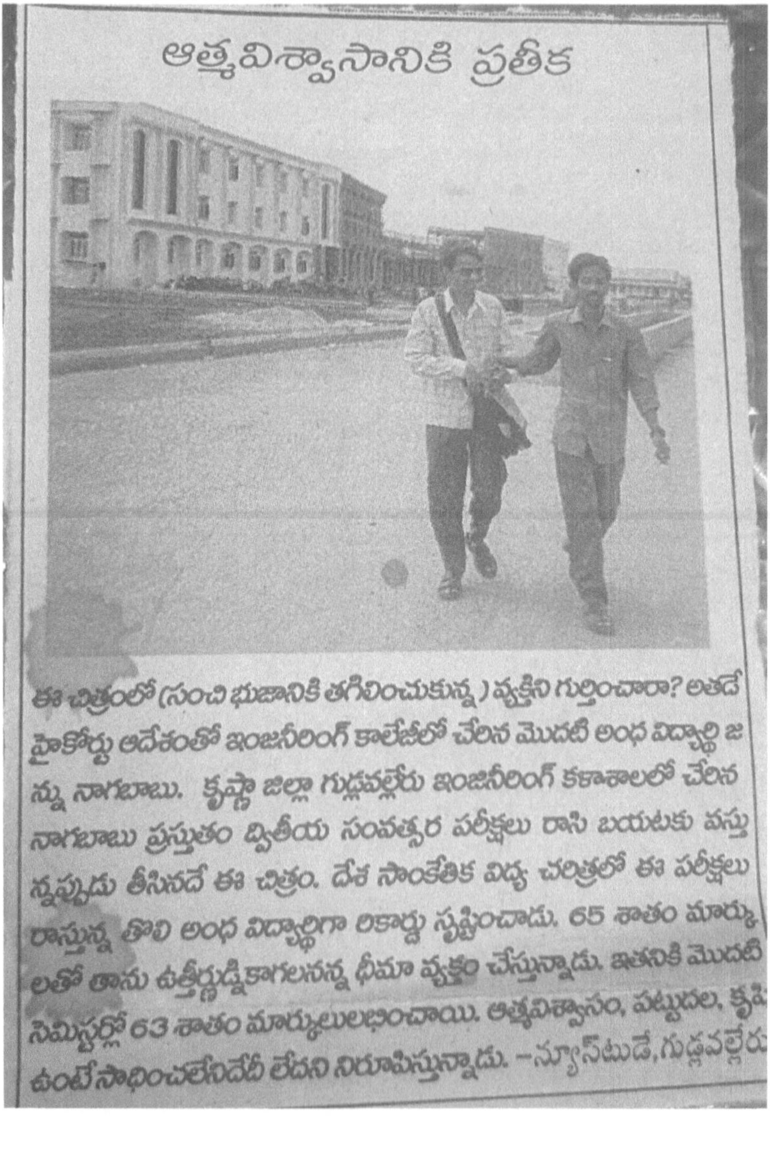

ఆత్మవిశ్వాసానికి ప్రతీక

ఈ చిత్రంలో (సంచి భుజానికి తగిలించుకున్న) వ్యక్తిని గుర్తించారా? అతడే హైకోర్టు ఆదేశంతో ఇంజనీరింగ్ కాలేజీలో చేరిన మొదటి అంధ విద్యార్థి జన్ను నాగబాబు. కృష్ణా జిల్లా గుడ్లవల్లేరు ఇంజినీరింగ్ కళాశాలలో చేరిన నాగబాబు ప్రస్తుతం ద్వితీయ సంవత్సర పరీక్షలు రాసి బయటకు వస్తున్నప్పుడు తీసినదే ఈ చిత్రం. దేశ సాంకేతిక విద్య చరిత్రలో ఈ పరీక్షలు రాస్తున్న తొలి అంధ విద్యార్థిగా రికార్డు సృష్టించాడు. 65 శాతం మార్కులతో తాను ఉత్తీర్ణుడ్నికాగలనన్న ధీమా వ్యక్తం చేస్తున్నాడు. ఇతనికి మొదటి సెమిస్టర్లో 63 శాతం మార్కులులభించాయి. ఆత్మవిశ్వాసం, పట్టుదల, కృషి ఉంటేసాధించలేనిదేదీ లేదని నిరూపిస్తున్నాడు. –న్యూస్‌టుడే,గుడ్లవల్లేరు

Fig 18: This article highlights my written test during Wipro campus placements, where my scribe supported me by helping me take the exam.

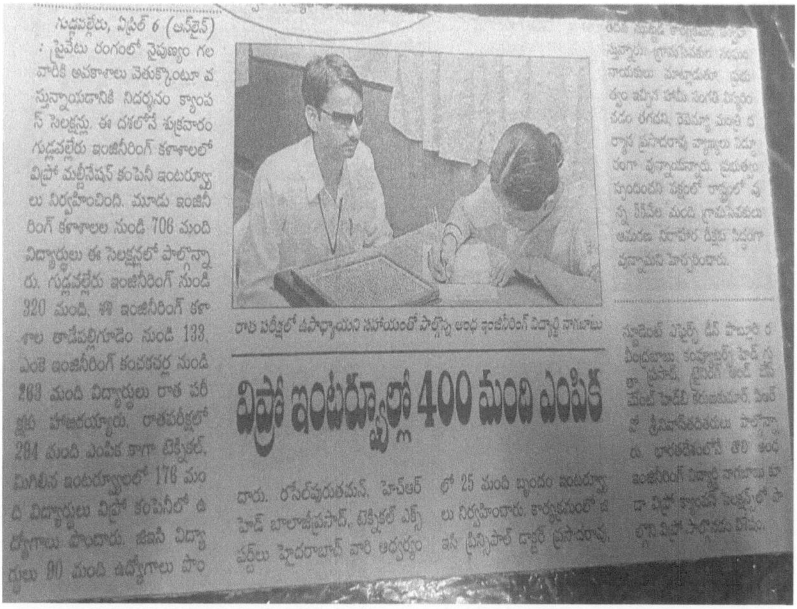

విప్రో ఇంటర్వ్యూల్లో 400 మంది ఎంపిక

రాత పరీక్షలో ఉపాధ్యాయుని సహాయంతో పాల్గొన్న అంధ ఇంజనీరింగ్ విద్యార్థి నాగబాబు

గుడ్లవల్లేరు, ఏప్రిల్ 6 (ఆన్‌లైన్) : ప్రైవేటు రంగంలో నైపుణ్యం గల వారికి అవకాశాలు వెతుక్కొంటూ వస్తున్నాయనడానికి నిదర్శనం క్యాంపస్ సెలక్షన్లు. ఈ దశలోనే శుక్రవారం గుడ్లవల్లేరు ఇంజనీరింగ్ కళాశాలలో విప్రో మల్టీనేషన్ కంపెనీ ఇంటర్వ్యూలు నిర్వహించింది. మూడు ఇంజనీరింగ్ కళాశాలల నుండి 706 మంది విద్యార్థులు ఈ సెలక్షన్లో పాల్గొన్నారు. గుడ్లవల్లేరు ఇంజనీరింగ్ నుండి 320 మంది, శ్రీ ఇంజనీరింగ్ కళాశాల తాడేపల్లిగూడెం నుండి 133, ఎంకె ఇంజనీరింగ్ కంచికచర్ల నుండి 263 మంది విద్యార్థులు రాత పరీక్షకు హాజరయ్యారు. రాతపరీక్షలో 294 మంది ఎంపిక కాగా టెక్నికల్, మిగిలిన ఇంటర్వ్యూలలో 176 మంది విద్యార్థులు విప్రో కంపెనీలో ఉద్యోగాలు పొందారు. జీవిసి విద్యార్థులు 90 మంది ఉద్యోగాలు పొందారు. రోసెల్‌పురుషమన్, హెచ్ఆర్ హెడ్ బాలాజీప్రసాద్, టెక్నికల్ ఎక్స్‌పర్ట్‌లు హైదరాబాద్ వారి ఆధ్వర్యంలో 25 మంది బృందం ఇంటర్వ్యూలు నిర్వహించారు. కార్యక్రమంలో జిఇసి ప్రిన్సిపాల్ డాక్టర్ ప్రసాదరావు, స్టూడెంట్ ఎఫైర్స్ డీన్ పొట్లూరి రవీంద్రబాబు, కంప్యూటర్స్ హెడ్ గుప్తా ప్రసాద్, ట్రైనింగ్ అండ్ ప్లేస్‌మెంట్ హెడ్ టి కరుణకుమార్, [illegible] పాల్గొన్నారు. భారతదేశంలోనే తొలి అంధ ఇంజనీరింగ్ విద్యార్థి నాగబాబు కూడా విప్రో క్యాంపస్ సెలక్షన్లలో పాల్గొని విప్రో [illegible] విశేషం.

Fig 19: Gudlavalleru College felicitated me for becoming the country's first blind diploma student to successfully earn an engineering degree.

భారత తొలి అంధ పాలిటెక్నిక్ విద్యార్థికి సత్కారం

భారతదేశ చరిత్రలోనే సంచలనం సృష్టించి గుడ్లవల్లేరు పాలిటెక్నిక్‌లో డిప్లమో చేసిన తొలి అంధ డిప్లమో విద్యార్థి జె నాగబాబును గుడ్లవల్లేరు పాలిటెక్నిక్ కళాశాల వారు సత్కరించారు. నాగబాబును ప్రోత్సహిస్తూ పూర్వవిద్యార్థి, ప్రవాస భారతీయుడు వెనిగెళ్ళ శ్రీనివాస్ రూ. ఐదువేలను బహుమతిగా అందచేశారు. అనంతరం ఇదే కళాశాలలో విద్యనభ్యసించిన మరో అంధ కంప్యూటర్ విద్యార్థి పవన్‌కుమార్‌కు కళాశాల వారిచే అంధులకోసం ప్రత్యేకంగా రూపొందించిన కంప్యూటర్ యుఎస్‌పి డ్రైవ్‌ను అందచేశారు.

అంధ విద్యార్థి నాగబాబును సత్కరిస్తున్న దృశ్యం

Epilogue: What the journey taught me

Looking back at the journey behind me, I see no turning point. No miracle moment. No instant when life was easy.

Instead, my story was shaped by a thousand steps, each one taken without sight but never without direction.

Every phase taught me something essential.

Blindness taught me resilience, poverty taught me hunger, rejection taught me courage, education taught me possibility, work taught me dignity, love taught me grounding, and illness taught me how to keep standing even when I don't know whether healing would come.

But the greatest lesson came quietly. That the world doesn't change when your circumstances improve. It changes when your vision deepens.

I once believed strength was about pushing through everything. Today, I know it is the opposite. Strength is the sum of every hand that held you, every voice that encouraged you, and every kindness that arrived without being asked.

I do not know what the next chapter will demand of my body or my mind. Every system I have learned made me understand that trust stands. Learning. Discipline. People. Patience. These have carried me this far, and they will carry me forward.

My life is not a story of overcoming blindness. It is a story of discovering a deeper kind of sight, one that grows from faith, purpose, persistence, and people.

The path ahead remains unseen. But I have learned something that cannot be taken away. I do not need to see the path to walk on it.

And if this journey proves anything, it is this. That life is never measured by what you see, but by how far you are willing to walk when the path disappears beneath your feet.

I didn't write this book to celebrate myself. I wrote it to remind anyone standing before a wall. Whether the walls are made of doubt, disability, or circumstance, they can be broken. Not always loudly, not always quickly. But always, always with courage.

And when you finally stand beyond that wall, you realize something profound.

The world wasn't waiting for you. You were waiting for yourself.

To connect with me, please visit:

https://www.nagababu.org/

www.ingramcontent.com/pod-product-compliance
Ingram Content Group UK Ltd.
Pitfield, Milton Keynes, MK11 3LW, UK
UKHW041351190726
13845UKWH00026B/538

9 789356 554078